INTENTIONAL

POWER

Lisen Stromberg
JeanAnn Nichols
Corey Jones

INTENTIONAL

POWER

The **6 Essential Leadership Skills** For
Triple Bottom Line Impact

WILEY

Published by John Wiley & Sons, Inc., Hoboken, New Jersey.
Published simultaneously in Canada.

For general information on our other products and services or for technical support, please contact our Customer Care Department within the United States at (800) 762-2974, outside the United States at (317) 572-3993 or fax (317) 572-4002.

Wiley also publishes its books in a variety of electronic formats. Some content that appears in print may not be available in electronic formats. For more information about Wiley products, visit our web site at www.wiley.com.

Library of Congress Cataloging-in-Publication Data is Available:

ISBN 9781394193509 (Cloth)
ISBN 9781394193516 (ePub)
ISBN 9781394193523 (ePDF)

Cover Design: Wiley

SKY10053856_082823

This work is dedicated to every Modern Leader who uses their power to benefit us all.

"Just as ripples spread out when a single pebble is dropped into water, the actions of individuals can have far-reaching effects."

—His Holiness, the Dalai Lama

Contents

The Modern Leader's Goal

Inspire free people, societies, and cultures to move courageously toward mutually beneficial positions where all can thrive.

The Modern Leader's Responsibility

Create and maintain environments that encourage confidence, creativity, and constructive change where all stakeholders prosper.

Preface

IF you, like us and like the thousands of leaders around the world with whom we have worked, coached, and collaborated, are realizing that everything has changed, that the old ways don't work anymore, and that we need a new model of leadership, then you are in the right place.

Welcome!

Intentional Power: The 6 Essential Leadership Skills for Triple Bottom Line Impact is for anyone who believes that their purpose as leaders—as humans—is to use what power they have in service to something far greater than just their company's bottom line. This book is for leaders who understand that work—and here we mean paid work—is central to our collective well-being, and so the places in which they work must support *all of us* to thrive. This book is for leaders who feel a sense of moral urgency because they recognize that the devastation of climate change won't just impact their lives but the lives of their children and grandchildren and the many generations that follow. This book is for leaders who see the potential of capitalism as a force for good, rather than as a force for the 1%.

Intentional Power is for leaders who are committed to delivering triple bottom-line impact—people, planet, and profits—because that is the *only way to lead* in this new world of work.

So if this sounds like you, thank you for giving us your precious time. Here's a little about us.

A month before the global lockdown, Lisen's mother died from a rare brain disease called PSP, or progressive supranuclear palsy. In many ways, her passing was a blessing given that it was both inevitable and timely. Lisen and her family were able to be in the hospital in those last days of her mother's life unlike so many whose loved ones died in hospitals alone because the pandemic limited access. The month before her mother's death, Lisen and JeanAnn, previously strangers, joined a small group of women committed to supporting each other professionally. Meanwhile, Lisen and Corey, who knew each other from previous work in advertising and marketing, began ideating how they could partner to help companies foster highly inclusive, highly productive, highly profitable workplace cultures—and then, Covid.

All three of us had recently left leadership roles at companies and were launching into new entrepreneurial careers. We were each on a mission to move from success to significance. What was supposed to be a professional connection, turned into a lasting collaboration to understand life, leadership, and the power of legacy.

Over the next six months, in the darkness that was the global pandemic, Corey, JeanAnn, and Lisen gathered virtually to try and make sense of the world. We bonded over our experiences as traditionally underrepresented talent in Corporate America and as humans. We pondered why it was so hard to thrive in the workplace, why companies—and their leaders—keep making the same mistakes when it comes to fostering cultures of belonging, and debated how companies could and should serve a purpose far greater than filling the bank accounts of a select few.

It didn't take long for us to realize we were aligned in our belief that the challenge was both rooted in, and could be solved by, focusing on leadership.

Our career journeys could not have been more different. After graduating from college with a degree in engineering and doing a one-year stint at National Semiconductor, JeanAnn built her career exploring the corporate jungle gym at one company, Intel. She started by working 12-hour night shifts in the manufacturing plant solving problems at 3:00 a.m. with a team of independent rebels. She made moves between product business units, communications, marketing, and sales groups honing her technical and business skills by leading global teams. The breadth of experiences served her well when she was appointed vice president and general manager, Sales and Marketing, leading Intel's Sales Enablement and Customer Experience organization with an $80B revenue pipeline. In that role, she also served on Intel's Ethics Compliance and Oversight Committee, providing the board of directors with insights to mitigate risks inherent in global corporate operations.

JeanAnn worked with leaders who were inspiring and supportive. Leaders who pushed her to grow and challenged her to expand her capabilities. She also worked with leaders whose leadership attitudes and behaviors were models of what to avoid. JeanAnn started at Intel the year Andy Grove was appointed CEO, and she thrived, in part, because of his leadership. A Hungarian Jew who escaped the Nazis, Andy inherently understood the plight of being "other," much like women are in the tech industry. He was renowned for his humility, believed in transparency, and proved his resilience in the face of challenge both personally and in his leadership of one of the tech industry's most successful companies. Andy is famous for coining the concept "Measure what matters," the foundation for venture capitalist John Doerr's book on the importance of objectives and key results (OKRs)—in other words, being accountable. Even though he led Intel in the latter decades of the 20th century, to JeanAnn, Andy Grove set an example for many elements of Modern Leadership.

Lisen's career has been decidedly nonlinear. After getting her MBA, she spent the next 15 years working in marketing and advertising. First, as a brand manager at the Nestle Corporation and then as a vice president at Foote, Cone, Belding—one of the largest advertising agencies in the United States. It was motherhood, or rather motherhood bias, that sent Lisen on a different path. Realizing that Corporate America abhorred caregivers and caregiving—it wants ideal workers who have no distractions and can be work devoted, thank you very much—Lisen became a "single shingle" marketing consultant working with Silicon Valley start-ups and a number of large tech companies as well. In her personal and professional life, she saw the same pattern again and again: highly skilled, ambitious women like herself who bumped up against leaders who couldn't, or wouldn't, support their dual identities as mothers and professionals.

Lisen ended up interviewing 186 women and surveyed over 1,500 more for her book, *Work, Pause, Thrive: How to Pause for Parenthood without Killing Your Career*. She learned about trailblazing women whose paths were not a direct route to the top. Unlike JeanAnn, these women twisted and turned and found their own path to success. Like Lisen and like JeanAnn, they faced #MeToo microaggressions, motherhood bias, and the challenge of being the "only" in the room. These women were the canaries in the coal mine indicating that something was not working at work. They proved to be harbingers for millennials and Gen Zs who, in recent years, have challenged leadership because they, too, see something is "rotten in Denmark."

As a creative and an innovator, Corey's career has centered on storytelling in and around the dynamic world of advertising. He has collaborated with and led teams that produced everything from digital technology, TV commercials, broadcast specials, and feature-length films to extensive digital installations and in-person activations that facilitated engagement and change for audiences all over the globe. Early in his career, Corey spent time creating content for T.D. Jakes and The Potter's House of Dallas, where every message tied purpose and leadership for better outcomes. It was there that Corey realized how important the actions and behaviors of leaders were to the communities that rely on them for growth and change.

Corey moved on to work in advertising, designing and delivering creative content for many brands you probably know. He experienced a few bumps including layoffs and stalled promotions along his circuitous journey to executive creative director, where he worked as one of only a handful of Black creative executives in that role across all agency holding companies in the US. Like so many people of color and other historically marginalized talent in the workplace, Corey experienced overt and hidden discrimination, but he also noticed something else. As the only person of color in the room of decision-makers, Corey found his approach to leadership differed from others who didn't share his experiences or perspective. He realized his teams always led in productivity, trust, and job satisfaction compared to other groups in those organizations. Corey understood microaggressions and the dark underbelly of living as the "other" in a white majority culture. He also understood that a new type of leadership was needed if people like him were going to not just survive but thrive in the workplace—and beyond.

And then Ahmaud Arbery, Breonna Taylor, George Floyd . . .

The horror facing Black Americans, the often inept response by company leaders to social and political upheaval, and the looming climate crisis fueled in us a sense of urgency. With JeanAnn serving as an advisor, Lisen and Corey launched PrismWork in 2020 in a world tilted sideways, but we saw disruption as an opportunity. This inspired us to ask, "What is a best-in-class Modern Leader? How do they foster workplace cultures that deliver on the triple bottom-line goals of people, planet, and profits? How can we support companies and leaders to make culture their competitive advantage?"

Our clients came to us asking for solutions, and so together we embarked on a journey to understand the core competencies of Modern Leadership. Our goal was to map those competencies to give leaders a new paradigm to meet the complexity of today's world.

We read scores of leadership books, listened to a myriad of podcasts, conducted extensive secondary research, and asked leaders themselves. We interviewed hundreds of women and men ranging from directors of engineering to vice presidents at manufacturing plants, from chief people officers at biotech firms to advertising CEOs, and then we surveyed thousands more. We wanted to unpack who was successful and why. Patterns emerged. Again and again we saw six core competencies rise to the top. Best-in-class leaders shared these traits and behaviors: humility, empathy, accountability, resiliency, transparency, and inclusivity. We call it the HEARTI® model—the six essential skills for Modern Leadership.

We wanted to test our philosophy around these new leadership competencies and decided what better place than to start with some of the smartest, next-gen talent struggling to lead in the midst of this century's biggest workplace disruption. In the fall of 2020, JeanAnn and Lisen offered our class on "Modern Leadership in the New World of Work" through Stanford University's continuing education program. It was, if we can say immodestly, a game changer.

We saw that the HEARTI model spoke to these leaders in ways previous leadership courses had not. Our students told us,

I finally have clarity on why it has been so challenging to lead before.

Now I know what I need to do.

You've provided me with a new way of showing up in the world.

This material should be provided to every person aiming to be a successful leader.

We have since taken HEARTI around the globe to leaders through our Modern Leadership labs, to teams through our group leadership programs, to international conferences, and to companies through speaking engagements, webinars, and coaching with their senior executives. As one of our students said, "This is isn't just about leading differently, this is a movement. Not just for our selves, but the world at large."

Our students asked for more, a guidebook to support their leadership journey long after they completed our course. This book was designed to meet their needs and yours. We start with context setting, putting words to the gestalt, and then lay out an overview of HEARTI to give you an understanding of the framework. At the heart of this book, we go deep into each of the six core competencies of HEARTI—humility, empathy, accountability, resiliency, transparency, and inclusivity—providing you with data, stories, and tools to help uplevel your leadership capabilities. We end with a call to purpose because why lead if you can't make an impact?

Thank you for the time you are committing to this book and for including us on your leadership journey. Most importantly, we are grateful to have you join the HEARTI movement and commit to making change for the generations to come.

1

Everything's Changed

WHEN their faces popped on to the screen as they joined our virtual classroom, you could see the eagerness and the anxiety. Thirty-seven students, mid-career professionals, had signed up for our winter 2023 Stanford Continuing Studies seminar on "Modern Leadership in the New World of Work." These up-and-coming leaders would be logging on to Zoom one night a week for the next eight weeks. In this class, like previous classes, we have students from around the world: San Francisco, New York, Toronto, London, Mumbai, Singapore, Jakarta, Sao Paulo, and many places in between. This means they'll be forced to stay up or wake up just to show up. And they do.

Why?

Much like the hundreds of students we have taught through Stanford and the thousands of leaders we engage with through our global leadership labs and our daily work, employees at every level are struggling with the complexity of today's new world of work. They, like all of us, are facing tectonic shifts in where, how, and even why we work. As one of our new students, Abel,* a senior director for a well-established tech company based in the San Francisco Bay Area shared, "I'm taking this class because I'm trying to understand how to be a good leader in the midst of this chaos."

Abel is zooming in from Atlanta. He moved back home mid-pandemic to be near family. Like him, his team of over 100 designers and engineers are now spread across the United States. Abel's boss wants everyone back in the office. He believes it will boost productivity, but Abel's teammates enjoy their new-found flexibility. He's already lost two high-performing employees to remote-first companies, and he worries he'll lose more if his company leaders stick to their plans. On top of that, with a looming recession, the company just cut funds for a deeply valued initiative: a program that offers technical skills training to minority students who can't afford a four-year college degree. His team is upset, morale is low. "I feel like I'm between a rock and a hard place," Abel admitted, bringing a vulnerability that is not unusual among our students.

Another student, a chief people officer for a fast-growing start-up, sympathized with Abel, "I'm taking this class because our managers are unsure how to lead in this environment. I need tools to help them."

At the beginning of each semester, we do our best to help our students put the challenges they are facing into context. We explain that to lead today, you need to understand the unprecedented forces that are putting pressure on companies and the people who run them. From employees who are challenging previous assumptions and expectations about the nature of work, to external stakeholders who are demanding companies step up to

---

*To protect our students' privacy, we won't be using their actual names throughout this book. Sometimes, like in the case of Abel, we'll create composite scenarios to ensure confidentiality, but rest assured these are real people doing their very best to lead with intention.

solve critical societal issues, to the underlying question of what is the essential purpose of a corporation, more is being asked of leaders than ever before.

It starts by understanding that *everything has changed.*

What Used to Work at Work No Longer Does

We don't need to belabor the reality that workplaces have seen a radical evolution these past few years. Global forces such as Covid-19, supply chain disruption, rampant inflation, rising interest rates, a labor shortage, and the threat of recession have amped up the stress level in today's businesses. Then, of course, the culture wars brought on by movements such as Black Lives Matter and #MeToo, the heightened political wedge between left and right, and the stark generational differences, only compound the disruption. Mashing together employees who bring different attitudes and beliefs about their relationship to work and the workplace has created a potential cauldron of cultural divisiveness.

Consider this: Millennials—those born between 1980 and 2000—already make up over 50% of the global workforce, and by 2025, Gen Z—those born between 1997 and 2012—will account for 27%.[1] As has been well-documented, millennials and Gen Zs see work through a very different lens than their predecessors. Rather than work-first, they are decidedly work-adjacent. In other words, work isn't their singular focus, it is part of the many things that make up their identity and only one of the things that gives them purpose.

Demographically, when combined, millennials and Gen Zs are the most diverse and the most educated workforce in history. Contrast this up-and-coming talent pool with the typical Fortune 500 CEO: Based on averages,[2] he's a man, around 60 years old, white, straight, and very likely has a spouse at home caring for the needs of the family. He has singularly devoted his life to rising up the corporate ladder and, in doing so, resembles the "ideal worker."[3] That's the person who is available at the drop of a hat, can work 24/7, and whose identity is defined by their job and title.

This ideal worker's experience in the midst of Covid has been decidedly different from the vast majority of his employees. A mid-pandemic study of over 31,000 knowledge workers worldwide revealed that 66% of them reported they were "struggling"—burned out, overworked, experiencing unprecedented levels of stress. Leaders? Nearly two in three said they were "thriving"—feeling more connected to their colleagues, earning more income, and enjoying increased time with family.[4]

This Covid chasm between leadership and employees has landed squarely on the shoulders of our students—next-gen leaders who are caught in the middle between old-school (we call them "Traditional") leaders who consider work to be their end-all be-all and are enjoying its benefits, and rising talent who definitely do not and are shouldering most of the load.

We've heard again and again in our research, "What used to work at work no longer does."

Old Way of Working:	New World of Work:
• Hierarchical	• Democratic
• Cultures of "What"	• Cultures of "Why"
• Facetime	• Results
• In-Person	• Work from Anywhere
• Homogenous	• Diverse
• Productivity-Focused	• People-Focused
• Profit over People	• Purpose, People, and Profits
• "Boomer" and "Gen Xer"	• "Millennial" and Emerging "Gen Z"

They're right. The traditional approach to how, where, and why we work has fundamentally shifted because of the significant internal and external demands on leaders, as well as the rapid pace of change. Businesses, and the leaders who run them, must either adapt or die. For instance, hierarchical, autocratic leadership is out; collaboration and democratic approaches are in. As we've seen from Abel and so many others, in-person, every day, all-day work is a failing strategy. Millennials and Gen Zs want more flexibility in the workplace, despite the dogged efforts of Traditional Leaders. And if your business focus is on productivity at all costs but lacks a clarity of purpose or mission, you probably already know that's a recipe for failure, sending employees into quiet quitting or loud resignations.

It's not just about *how* we work that is under fire, it's about *why*. Today's employees and job seekers want more from work than a paycheck, they want to work to be the vehicle through which they can make an impact on the world. They want their companies to be driven by more than the bottom line.

And it's not just employees demanding change. It is consumers, too. A recent study surveying 8,000 individuals across eight global markets revealed that consumers are four times more likely to buy from a company that they perceive as purpose-driven. And if they didn't think the company was "walking the talk," 76% said they took action including no longer buying from the brand, switching to a competitor, or discouraging others from buying from or supporting that brand.[5]

The expectation on business as a tool for social good has increased significantly over the last five years. Public relations powerhouse Edelman reported in a recent study that 70% of consumers wanted the brands they buy to address social and environmental issues. The report revealed that business is now the sole institution seen as competent and ethical; government is viewed as unethical and incompetent. Meanwhile, six times as many respondents said business is not doing enough (vs. overstepping) on societal issues such as climate change, economic inequality, energy shortages, health care access, and reskilling the workforce.[6]

This puts leaders, as Abel made clear, between a rock and a hard place. Why? Because the stakes have never been greater for leaders like himself to improve the overall health of the business, all the while satisfying increased employee expectations for meaning, purpose, inclusion, and societal good.

The purpose of the corporation must evolve, but Traditional Leaders are struggling to adapt.

Corporate Purpose: It's Not (Only) Profits

A brief history of corporate purpose reveals that sentiments have swung back and forth over the past 100 years. In the early days of the 20th century, companies were exclusively focused on profits, but by the mid-20th century opinions had changed. In 1957, Harvard economist Carl Kaysen wrote that management should see "itself as responsible to stockholders, employees, customers, the general public, and, perhaps most important, the firm itself as an institution."[7] However, all of that changed in 1970 when economist Milton Friedman redefined the role of the corporation to be exclusively focused on shareholder value.[8] His philosophy became embedded into how companies have been run these past 50 years. This means every decision made by a leader has been designed to ensure profits for the company and, by implication, money for the shareholder.

For some current context regarding those shareholders, 1% of investors own a majority of the stocks in the US stock market, and since 2020, that 1% gained nearly two-thirds of the $42B in new wealth creation.[9] According to the World Bank, we are experiencing the biggest increase in global inequality and poverty since World War II.[10] We also face the single biggest existential crisis of our time in the potentially devastating impact of climate change. As the rich have gotten richer and the rest have struggled to make do while the looming climate crises went from a theoretical debate to a daily reality, attitudes regarding the role of the corporation have changed. Employees, customers, consumers, and even investors have been asking themselves, "Given all of its power, shouldn't a company do more than make the 1% richer?"

> *Without question, the balance of power on the planet today lies in the hands of business. Corporations rival governments in wealth, influence, and power. . . . If a values-driven approach to business can begin to redirect this vast power toward more constructive ends than the simple accumulation of wealth, the human race and Planet Earth will have a fighting chance.*
> **—Ben Cohen, founder of Ben & Jerry's Ice Cream[11]**

Hamdi Ulukay, CEO of yogurt maker Chobani, thinks so. He came to the United States from Turkey to study English in upstate New York. He'd heard about a Kraft food plant closing in the area leaving hundreds of long-time employees jobless. Hamdi was furious. How could the company abandon these loyal workers?! With no money and no business experience, Hamdi managed to raise the funds to buy the plant. Within a year he was able to hire back all of the employees who had been fired and eventually hundreds more.

Hamdi decided his company's purpose was to provide meaningful jobs and create a workplace culture of inclusion and belonging where the employees, their families, and the communities in which they live thrive. Today, Chobani employs over 2,000 women and men; 38% are minorities, 30% are refugees. His executive team is 50% women, and each and every employee is an owner of the company.

In 2019 Hamdi took the stage at TED and declared, "We need a new playbook that sees people . . . above and beyond profits." Hamdi told the TED audience, "If you are right with your people, right with your community, and right with your product, you will be more profitable, more innovative, and have more passionate people who work for you, and a community that supports you."[12]

Even investors have been rethinking the purpose of the corporation. In his 2022 annual letter to CEOs, Larry Fink, CEO of Blackrock, one of the world's largest asset managers, declared, "The pandemic has turbocharged an evolution in the operating environment for virtually every company. . . . And the relationship between a company, its employees, and society is being redefined. A company must create value for and be valued by its full range of stakeholders in order to deliver long-term value for its shareholders."[13]

Pressures from consumers, employees, and investors among others has forced Corporate America to take notice—and take action. In 2019 the Business Roundtable, an association of 181 CEOs who run the largest US-based corporations, announced the purpose of a corporation should no longer be exclusively about shareholder value—now it would be about stakeholder value.

Their announcement read:

We commit to:

- Delivering value to our customers. We will further the tradition of American companies leading the way in meeting or exceeding customer expectations.
- Investing in our employees. This starts with compensating them fairly and providing important benefits. It also includes supporting them through training and education that help develop new skills for a rapidly changing world. We foster diversity and inclusion, dignity and respect.
- Dealing fairly and ethically with our suppliers. We are dedicated to serving as good partners to the other companies, large and small, that help us meet our missions.

- Supporting the communities in which we work. We respect the people in our communities and protect the environment by embracing sustainable practices across our businesses.
- Generating long-term value for shareholders, who provide the capital that allows companies to invest, grow and innovate. We are committed to transparency and effective engagement with shareholders.

They finished the announcement with this:

Each of our stakeholders is essential. We commit to deliver value to all of them, for the future success of our companies, our communities and our country.[14]

This new statement affirms the essential role corporations can play in improving our society when CEOs are truly committed to meeting the needs of all stakeholders.

—Alex Gorsky, CEO of Johnson & Johnson and chair of the Business Roundtable's corporate governance committee[15]

The move by the Business Roundtable was a clarion call for change.

From Shareholder to Stakeholder Capitalism

Capitalism as we have known it is dead. This obsession that we have with maximizing profits for shareholders alone has led to incredible inequity and a planetary emergency.

—Marc Benioff, CEO of SalesForce[16]

For far too long, leaders and shareholders have argued that a singular focus on delivering profits for investors was the only way to ensure optimal financial outcomes. But broader stakeholder capitalism is challenging that approach. Let's start with some definitions:

Shareholder capitalism (aka "me-first" capitalism) is a system that is rooted in the belief that the sole purpose of the corporation is to provide value to shareholders. This means the sole purpose of the leaders within that corporation is to focus on productivity, output, with a relentless focus on limiting expenses to ensure the singular bottom line delivers as much profit as possible.

Stakeholder capitalism (aka "we-first capitalism) is a system in which corporations are oriented to serve the interests of *all* their stakeholders. Among the key stakeholders are customers, suppliers, employees, shareholders, local communities, and the planet as a whole. The responsibility of leaders becomes broader than a singular bottom line. Their success and the success of the company expands to consider the people they serve (from employees to the communities in which it operates), to the consequences of the company operations on the planet, along with ensuring shareholder profitability. It's about shifting focus from the singular bottom line to the triple bottom line (people, planet, profits).

Stakeholder capitalism is not about politics. It is not a social or ideological agenda. It is not "woke." It is capitalism, driven by mutually beneficial relationships between you and the employees, customers, suppliers, and communities your company relies on to prosper. This is the power of capitalism.

—**Larry Fink, CEO of Blackrock, in his 2022 letter to CEOs**[17]

This triple bottom-line approach is one that Ginni Rometty, former CEO of IBM and a member of the Business Roundtable who established the new rules for corporate purpose, admitted "seemed so obvious to us" when she spoke to a ballroom-sized audience at SXSW in March 2023. "We were just formalizing what we had been doing for years."

Triple Bottom-Line Impact = #DoingWellByDoingGood

What exactly is the triple bottom line (3BL)? It has been defined as "a sustainability framework that measures a business's success in three key areas: people, planet, and profit."

Let's break it down even further:

- **People:** the positive and negative impact an organization has on its most important stakeholders. These include employees, families, customers, suppliers, communities, and any other person influencing or being affected by the organization.
- **Planet:** the positive and negative impact an organization has on its natural environment. This includes reducing its carbon footprint, usage of natural resources, emission of toxic materials, and so on but also the active removal of waste and reforestation and restoration of the natural environment.
- **Profit:** the positive and negative impact an organization has on the local, national, and international economy. This includes creating employment, generating innovation, paying taxes, creating wealth, delivering value to shareholders, and any other economic impact of the organization.

So how does a 3BL approach show up in the day-to-day? A great example is the One Planet initiative at chemical giant Solvay.

When Ilham Kadri became CEO of chemical giant Solvay, she was already aligned with the sustainability goals mapped out by the United Nations and in 2020 launched the Solvay One Planet initiative. "As a chemical company we can be part of the problem or part of the solution. We chose to be part of the solution," she said when the announcement was made.[18]

Solvay's One Planet has a three-pronged focus to make a positive impact on climate, resources, and a better life for its employees. Efforts include doubling the rate at which it reduces emissions, with a goal of curbing greenhouse gas emissions by 26% by 2030, reducing by a third its non-recoverable industrial waste, such as landfill and incineration without energy recovery, and expanding its global parental leave to 16 weeks for all new parents. While you might think these initiatives would be a drag on profits, in fact, profits have grown 21% since Ilham took the helm in 2016.[19] #DoingWellByDoingGood

The companies that put sustainability at their core are the ones that outlast and outperform the competition.

—Ilham Kadri, CEO of Solvay[20]

You Need to Know

The Seven Core Elements of a 3BL Company

1) A strong, publicly stated set of values
2) Ethical and sustainable business practices
3) Ongoing and continuous support for important social causes

4) Products and services that reflect the needs of people today

5) Commitment to, and support of, the communities in which the company operates

6) Fair and equitable programs, policies, and practices

7) Diverse and inclusive workplace culture

Another example is Gina Mastantuono, the chief financial officer of ServiceNow, a cloud computing platform based in Silicon Valley. She's passionate about ESG (see the box for information on ESG). In 2021, the company published their first Global Impact Report supporting Gina's objective to create long-term value. ServiceNow set ESG goals to sustain the planet, provide equitable opportunity, and act with integrity. They committed to specific goals and created a process to capture and analyze, implement, and reduce on each of the vectors. In two years, they've achieved 100% renewable electricity and carbon neutrality, distributed $100M through their Racial Equity Fund, and invested $10M+ in local communities.

ServiceNow is being transparent about where they are today and humbly reports that they're just starting their journey. As Gina said, "Given ESG's connection to long-term value creation, we've made it a strategic imperative, embedding it into our operations, solutions, and cultural mindset to benefit our employees, customers, partners, and communities."[21] Since she started in January of 2020, the company's revenues have increased 64%. #DoingWellByDoingGood

But let's be clear: 3BL is not just some new way to do accounting or some external metric to measure company actions. It is about operating with an underlying belief that long-term sustainable impact to the betterment of our world is THE role of the corporation. And, it's about sustainable change that aims to deliver prosperity for *all* stakeholders.

Triple Bottom-Line Impact

You Need to Know

The Link between ESG and 3BL

What is ESG? It stands for environmental, social, and governance. In brief, ESG is a way to keep companies accountable for how they conduct their businesses and is a framework that serves leaders committed to 3BL impact.

The environmental component is driven by sustainable efforts to insure companies are reducing impact on the environment from their carbon footprint, water usage, waste, and product recyclability. The social component covers the myriad of ways companies interact with their employees and the communities in which they operate. The governance component considers the systems and processes a company has in place to ensure ethical govern-ance including pay equity, executive compensation, audit-ing, and more. ESG is the triple bottom line: the planet (E), people (S), and profits (G).

In the past decade, investing based on ESG metrics has soared. ESG assets under management are set to reach over $50 trillion by 2025, according to Bloomberg. That's a third of total assets under management.[22] Why? Because it's good for business. More than 2,000 academic studies have exam-ined the impact of environmental, social, and governance propositions on equity returns, and 63% of them found positive results (versus only 8% that were negative).[23]

Prosperity for All

Sounds good, but what does it really mean? The current defi-nition of prosperity focuses on wealth. The Oxford Dictionary defines it as "flourishing financially," so it is no wonder that when we talk about prosperity we, as leaders, often think it is about profits. But the origins of the word prosperity come from both Latin and Greek where the focus is less on economics and more on overall well-being.

Prosperity is about thriving.

So when we talk about prosperity for all, we're not just talk-ing about everyone's financial well-being. It's about fostering a world in which humans are safe, healthy, and secure and where each of us can thrive today and in the many decades to come.

The United Nations 2030 Agenda for Sustainable Develop-ment, which aims to bring prosperity to all nations, has mapped out the following goals for the world:

- We are determined to end poverty and hunger, in all their forms and dimensions, and to ensure that all human beings can fulfill their potential in dignity and equality and in a healthy environment.

- We are determined to protect the planet from degradation, including through sustainable consumption and production, sustainably managing its natural resources and taking urgent action on climate change, so that it can support the needs of the present and future generations.
- We are determined to ensure that all human beings can enjoy prosperous and fulfilling lives and that economic, social and technological progress occurs in harmony with nature.
- We are determined to foster peaceful, just, and inclusive societies which are free from fear and violence. There can be no sustainable development without peace and no peace without sustainable development.[24]

Now that is prosperity for all!

Everett Harper, CEO of Truss, an Inc. 5000 fastest-growing company, writes in his book, *Move to the Edge, Declare it Center: Practices and Process for Creatively Solving Complex Problems,* "We have urgent, complex challenges to address, and 20th-century tools [and behaviors] don't work for 21st-century problems. Leaders need to approach today's complex systems with a different mindset—led by curiosity and experimentation."[25]

Today's best leaders strive to operate with a triple bottom line approach that benefits people, the planet, and delivers profits to the shareholders.

Our students have that urgency, that curiosity, and that willingness to try new approaches. Why? Because they, like you, understand that everything has changed and know that the answer to the complex and grave problems facing our world today requires a different approach to leadership, one that is rooted in the deep belief that driving for prosperity for all over one's own self-interest is how to make a positive impact in the world at large.

You Need to Know

The New World of Work in Context

1) The generational and demographic differences in today's workplace require a new kind of leadership.

2) Consumers, customers, suppliers, employees, community members, and investors are all demanding leaders put their skills, abilities, power, and position toward helping solve society's biggest problems.

3) The purpose of the corporation has shifted from a singular short-term focus on shareholder capitalism to the wider and longer-term focus of serving broader stakeholder capitalism.

4) Linking a triple bottom line approach to business success is foundational to delivering on the promise of the modern corporation's purpose.

5) To succeed in the new world of work, modern companies—and the leaders who run them—must be driven by long-term impact that delivers prosperity for all.

2

Intentional Power Skills for Stakeholder Success

REMEMBER the quiet of the global pandemic lockdown? The way traffic was silenced—no cars, no buses, no trains, no planes—which meant birds could be heard as they haven't for years. For those of us who weren't on the frontlines (and blessings of gratitude for those heroes who were), an unexpected silence became the collective reality. Within that silence, we three began to wonder if THIS was the moment companies and their leaders would, finally, wake up and change.

We launched PrismWork in the middle of 2020 as companies and their leaders scrambled to figure out a new operating system for the workplace. The PrismWork founders and our consulting partners came together with a shared vision for fostering sustainable workplaces that would deliver on the promise of the triple bottom line. We have partnered with clients who understand that widening the lens to include people, planet, and profits is essential for their company's success and that having a triple bottom-line approach is key to future-proofing their companies.

Early clients included a fast-growing start-up that wanted to "get culture right" so it was built to last, a decades-old company led by a CEO who was surprised to learn many on his own leadership team did not feel a sense of inclusion or belonging, and a well-established mid-tier company with a new chief people officer who saw the pandemic as a chance to reinforce or remake their company's culture. Other clients included industry associations, global Fortune 500 companies, advertising agencies, and venture capital firms. What they all had in common was a recognition that the world has changed and the way they lead must change, too.

We're proud of the good work we did with these companies, but we also saw patterns that prevented many of them from truly achieving their ambitious goals. We spoke to leaders who boasted they were committed to hiring previously under-recognized talent but who made no real effort to reshape the behaviors, systems, policies, or programs that had kept the diverse talent pool away in the first place. We spoke to other leaders who professed a commitment to fostering inclusive cultures but whose leadership teams remained white and male and who told us, "There just aren't enough women/Blacks/Latines/LGBTQ+ (name the traditionally marginalized group) to hire." We spoke to leaders who believed that peak productivity could only be achieved if employees were within eyesight and wanted to get their employees "back to work"—as though these very employees weren't actually *working* while locked in their homes during Covid. And, we spoke to leaders who were struggling with the generational differences. As one admitted to us, "I know my younger employees mean well, but they never seem satisfied. Their expectations are so high. It feels like entitlement to me."

Each of the leaders we spoke to told us they wanted to create thriving, sustainable cultures grounded in inclusion and belonging, but their actions revealed an aspiration-action gap. In truth, they weren't willing, or able, to do the self-discovery and hard culture work necessary to create the companies and cultures they claimed they wanted. They're not alone.

Moving from "Me" to "We"

In 2005, novelist and essayist David Foster Wallace gave a now famous commencement speech to the graduating class of Kenyon College. He called it, "This is Water."[1] He started his speech with this parable: *There are these two young fish swimming along, and they happen to meet an older fish swimming the other way, who nods at them and says, "Morning, boys. How's the water?" And the two young fish swim on for a bit, and then eventually one of them looks over at the other and goes "What the hell is water?"*

When we share this story with our students and clients, we explain that in the United States, and many other countries around the world, we have been swimming in the water of "boot-strap individualism." It's the notion that one's individual success is due to their individual efforts. In the workplace it becomes about advancing one's individual goals and priorities over the needs of others. Individualism is rooted in a "me" mindset and is a philosophy so deeply embedded most of us don't even know it's water.

But the water is murky. As we discussed in Chapter 1, "Everything's Changed," shareholder capitalism has been at the core of how companies have been led these past five decades. It fosters a "winner take all" approach to leadership and succeeds when leaders operate with a "me" mindset. This type of capitalism has led to deep inequities in society and, many would argue, is one of the key reasons our planet is in crisis.

We now know from research that leaders who serve more than a single stakeholder are held in higher regard than their counterparts. For CEOs whose sole focus was on shareholder value, followers were more likely to view the CEO as autocratic. But, when the CEO took a 3BL approach emphasizing stakeholder values, followers were more likely to view them as visionary leaders.[2] And here is the key: When employees saw their leaders as visionary, they expended more effort, and their companies saw increased financial performance. In other words, the

Shifting from shareholder capitalism to stakeholder capitalism requires a completely new approach to leadership.

stakeholder approach is better for the bottom line.

Traditional Leaders who are devotees of shareholder capitalism operate from a hierarchical, centralized, my-way-or-the-highway approach with a focus on profits, usually at the expense of people. Employees are viewed as replaceable and seen primarily in terms of their ability to be of use to the bottom line. Traditional Leaders create workplace cultures that are highly competitive and often lead to burnout as employees try to outgun each other and "win." It's an industrial age, command-and-control approach to leadership that comes right out of the 20th century military, a model that even today's United States Army has rejected as a recipe for failure.

In 2019, the US Army authored a 62-page report on Modern Leadership. It details counterproductive mindsets and cautions against high-risk leadership behaviors "that result from self-centered motivations on the part of the leader, where they act in ways that seek primarily to accomplish their own goals and needs before those of others." The report states that "the most effective leaders . . . are open to feedback from others and actively seek it. [They] work toward something more important than themselves."[3]

At PrismWork, our experience is that the best-in-class leaders of today (we call them Modern Leaders) have a "we" mindset rooted in the belief that the purpose of a corporation goes beyond exclusively delivering results for the single bottom line and that their role as leaders is far greater than enhancing shareholder profits. These Modern Leaders are serving broader stakeholder interests (hence, the term stakeholder capitalism). They are committed to driving outcomes for the benefit of people, the planet, *and* profits as the collective measurement of success.

As the Army makes clear, Modern Leaders understand their success is tied to the success of their teams. They are people-focused, collaborative, and empower their employees by trusting them to make the decisions necessary to support themselves, their colleagues, and the company overall. Modern Leaders work to ensure their teams connect the day-to-day activities of the company to an overall purpose that benefits not just the company, but the world at large.

To deliver triple bottom-line impact leaders must move from a "me" mindset to a "we" mindset.

Modern Leaders have ambitions far greater than their personal goals; they are focused on making an impact that benefits generations to come.

Traditional "Me" Leadership	Modern "We" Leadership
• Authoritarian/command and control	• Authoritative/collaborative
• "Leader's command" (centralized decision-making)	• "Leader's intent" (decentralized decision-making)
• "Get it done fast"	• "Get it done right"
• Driven by scarcity (fixed mindset)	• Driven by abundance (growth mindset)
• Guarded	• Transparent
• Arrogant	• Humble
• Single-minded (micro-manages)	• Visionary (delegates)
• Profits, profits, and profits (shareholder capitalism)	• Purpose, people, planet, and profits (stakeholder capitalism)

Redefining Leadership

Below we provide some context for what it means to move from a traditional leader to a modern leader.

I believe that every company and every individual—from new hires to those sitting in the corner office—has the potential to become a platform for change. Not only because it is the right thing to do, but also because in the future, success will demand it.

—Marc Benioff, CEO, Salesforce and coauthor,
Trailblazer: The Power of Business as the Greatest Platform for Change[4]

Masters of Modern Leadership

So how does a Modern Leader show up differently? Consider these two examples:

For many, Yvon Chouinard is the paragon of a Modern Leader who is committed to the long-term benefit of all stakeholders. He founded Patagonia in 1973. Yvon grew the company to over $1 billion in revenue with a focus on the triple bottom line of people, planet, and profit. Patagonia's consistent focus on sustainability is seen in the mission statement: "We're in business to save our home planet."[5]

Operationally, this has meant that the company has pioneered the use of recycled materials in new products and committed to 100% renewable energy within the United States and 76% globally, launching a program called "Worn Wear" to extend the life cycle of their products, offering used gear, and allowing consumers to trade in or repair their used Patagonia gear. A forward-thinking approach to employee engagement has ensured an inclusive culture through programs including onsite daycare, a relentless commitment to pay equity, and a fair-trade commitment for their supplier's factory workers. The company has been transparent in their approach to public activism by enabling employees to use retail spaces after hours for social and political volunteer efforts. They also spearheaded a $1 million campaign to get out the vote in 2016 and closed stores to allow employees and shoppers to go to polling stations and cast their votes.

In late 2022, Yvon Chouinard and his family decided to transfer their entire ownership stake into two novel entities to ensure their values will be upheld long after their involvement in the company ends.[6] The nonprofit Holdfast Collective will use the company's annual profits, about $100 million per year, to "protect nature and biodiversity, support thriving communities and fight the environmental crisis." The Patagonia Purpose Trust will create a permanent legal structure so that the company can never stray from Chouinard's vision that a for-profit business can work for the planet. Why? Because as he says, "If we have any hope of a thriving planet 50 years from now, it demands all of us doing all we can with the resources we have."

Earth is now our only shareholder.

—Yvon Chouinard, founder Patagonia[7]

Not every leader will be Yvon Chouinard, and not every company will be as future-forward as Patagonia, but there are many, many examples of leaders who have risen through the ranks to achieve significant impact for people, planet, and profits. Consider former PepsiCo Chairman and CEO Indra Nooyi, who used her power with intention to drive change within the organization to the benefit of the company, its customers, and the communities in which it operates.

Over the 12 years of Indra's tenure as CEO, PepsiCo delivered measurable results on product, planet, people, and profit, including:

- PepsiCo's portfolio of healthier options grew from about 38% of revenue in 2006 to roughly 50% in 2017. PepsiCo and other leading food and beverage companies offered consumers reformulated products and smaller serving sizes, removing six trillion calories from their products.
- Water use by its operations was reduced by 25% from 2006 to 2018 and PepsiCo provided safe drinking water to

22 million citizens in the communities it served. The company's environmental sustainability projects have saved the company $600+ million.

■ Women held 39% of senior management roles by 2018.

■ Net revenue grew at an annualized rate of 5.5%, reaching $63.5 billion in 2017, and PepsiCo stock outperformed both the Consumer Staples Select Sector Index and the S&P 500.[8]

How did Indra do it? Under an initiative she launched called "Performance with Purpose (PwP)," PepsiCo committed to deliver excellent performance, as was expected by fiduciary stakeholders, but added three imperatives to the work ahead.

1) **Human Benefit:** transforming the product portfolio by reducing the sugar, salt, and fat in its products while dialing up more healthful, more nutritious foods and beverages;

2) **Environmental Improvement:** limiting its environmental impact by conserving water and reducing PepsiCo's carbon footprint and plastic waste;

3) **Talent Evolution:** lifting people by offering new types of support to women and families inside the company and in the communities PepsiCo serves.[9]

PwP was not corporate social responsibility or philanthropy but rather a way to transform PepsiCo's approach to the bottom line—from shareholders to stakeholders. If the company didn't meet changing consumer tastes, it couldn't grow. If the company failed to manage its operations impact on the environment, costs would rise. If the company didn't encourage people to bring their whole selves to work, they wouldn't attract the best employees. Altogether, if the company didn't deliver performance, it couldn't fund its purpose.

Indra reflects, "I look back at PepsiCo and am proud of the company it is today and will be in the future. It has succeeded both commercially and ethically. It has learned to balance the short term and the long term, carefully thinking through the level and the duration of returns. A real sense of purpose is integrated into the company's core operations. So to anyone who doubts whether it's possible to build such a company, I say, 'We did it at PepsiCo, and you can do it too.' It's the only way to make capitalism work for everyone."

> *The success of any business is inextricably linked to the sustainability of the world around us.*
>
> **—Indra Nooyi, former CEO of PepsiCo**[10]

Intentional Power

As we have shared, in our experience many of the challenges leaders are facing today are a result of the struggle to move from shareholder (me-first) to stakeholder (we-first) capitalism and from Traditional Leadership to Modern Leadership. Doing this takes work. It starts with a fundamental shift in mindset.

It was a near-death experience that jolted Clarke Murphy to intentionally shift his mindset and become a champion for triple bottom-line impact. Clarke spent the majority of his career at premier executive recruiting firm Russell Reynolds, eventually rising to become CEO. When he wasn't working, Clarke was sailing, a passion he developed as a young boy growing up in a large Irish-Catholic family in Virginia, just outside of Washington, DC.

In 2015, he was racing in the middle of the North Atlantic Ocean trying to maneuver in pea-soup fog when he suddenly saw a 40-foot container floating just below the surface. At the speed they were going, a dead-on hit would have sunk the boat in less than five minutes. Quick action saved him and his crewmates, but the experience changed Clarke forever. He realized the trash floating in our oceans might not have killed him that day but would kill our world eventually. He said, "Seeing the changes in our oceans, and for me almost dying because of it, that's when I knew, 'I've got to do something.'"

In January 2023, we invited Clarke to be a guest speaker at a virtual summit hosted by PrismWork. As we prepped for the event, Clarke shared that before this epiphany happened, he wasn't really focused on sustainability as foundational to best-in-class leadership. But once he "saw the future," helping leaders shift their mindsets so they can truly understand the importance of a stakeholder approach focused on long-term sustainability became Clarke's mission.

As Clarke explains in his book, *Sustainable Leadership: Lesson of Vision, Courage, and Grit From the CEOs Who Dared to Build a Better World*, today's most successful, future-forward leaders operate with a "purpose-driven belief that business is not just a commercial activity divorced from the wider societal and environmental context in which it operates."[11] He and his team at Russell Reynolds interviewed and surveyed thousands of women and men to understand if, and how, today's leaders are operating with sustainability as their leadership focus. He learned that sustainable leaders have a "strong mandate to step up, fill the void, and lead on broader societal issues that go far beyond their corporate footprints." Clarke says that to be successful in today's complex world, a "leader must manage and innovate for commercial, environmental, and social outcomes."

> *The great leaders of the future will balance operating profit with sustainable leadership . . . including fostering cultures that benefit **all** stakeholders.*
>
> **—Clarke Murphy, former CEO**
> **Russell Reynolds and Associates**

Clarke and the leaders he writes about in his book have one thing in common: they use their power to lead with intention.

Deepa Purushothaman is another Modern Leader who shifted her mindset and is using her power with intention. She was one of the youngest people and first Indian American woman to be named partner at the prestigious consulting firm Deloitte. She spent 20 years climbing the corporate ladder and, by all outward appearances, succeeded. But the years working in a system driven by shareholder capitalism were hard on her physical and emotional health and her overall well-being. Eventually, Deepa had had enough. She decided it was time to challenge and redefine the status quo of leadership, success, and power, so she pivoted her career. Today, she is an author, speaker, and Executive Fellow at Harvard Business School.

In her debut book, *The First, the Few, the Only: How Women of Color Can Redefine Power in Corporate America*, Deepa writes, "In our capitalist society, where white men have gained advantage and wealth by exerting power over others, we have been taught that this is the path to success. It's a game based on scarcity, competition, and winner takes all."[12]

When it comes to Corporate America, Deepa has a point. You've read the stats: men outnumber women five to one in senior leadership positions in Corporate America overall and make up 83% of the C-suite in the S&P's top 100 companies. As for detail on these men, Black men held 19 named executive officer positions in 2022, up from 14 in 2020, five CEOs out of the Fortune 500 are Latino men and seven are Asian men. According to executive search firm Heidrick & Struggles, Fortune 500 boards have actually "taken a step back when it comes to diversity." The company's 2023 Board Monitor US report notes that in 2022, 40% of Fortune 500 new director seats went to women, down from 45% in 2021, and 34% went to racial or ethnic minorities, down from 41% in 2021.[13] In other words, white men (still) make up the vast majority of leaders in power across Corporate America.

To create a more equitable workplace and world, Deepa believes we need a new playbook for success, one rooted in a new definition of power that's required to lead with intention.

New power is about how we see the past and our future and how we take responsibility for what is next.

—**Deepa Purushothaman, thought leader and author of *The First, the Few, the Only: How Women of Color Can Redefine Power in Corporate America.*[14]**

You Need to Know

Redefining Power

Traditional Power is part of a me-first approach to leadership. It:

- Focuses on domination and control (power "over");
- Maintains the status quo;
- Limits empathy and collaboration;
- Rewards self-serving behavior;
- Reinforces a belief in exceptionalism.

Intentional Power is essential to a we-first approach to leadership. It:

- Focuses on influence and impact (power "in partnership with");
- Creates more equitable systems and rewards;
- Promotes civility and respect;
- Rewards collaboration;
- Reinforces a belief in community and collective action.

You never change things by fighting the existing reality. To change something, build a new model that makes the existing model obsolete.

—**R. Buckminster Fuller**

HEARTI: The Six Essential Skills for Modern Leaders

Here's the thing: Modern Leaders who want to use their power with the intention of driving long-term sustainable results need a new set of skills. Why? Because the way leaders have been evaluated, rewarded, promoted, and even simply recognized is no longer viable in a broader stakeholder approach to success.

In the past, leaders deemed as effective were identified by their command and control of people and operations. They had hard skills such as technical and financial acumen that were seen as primary to their success. Their soft skills (aka: people skills) were viewed through the lens of old power and shareholder capitalism. In other words, how many employees could you coerce to be work-devoted to achieve your profit goals? In this environment, the soft skills that were valued included decisiveness, aggressiveness, independence, dominance, analytical/logical thinking, competitive spirit, and so on. Leaders who mastered these soft skills thrived in the old power, shareholder-capitalist environment.

John Gerzema, co-CEO of the Harris Poll and coauthor of *The Athena Doctrine: How Women (and the Men Who Think Like Them) Will Rule the Future,* knows old power "soft" skills don't work today. He surveyed and interviewed 64,000 leaders around the world to understand the core skills of Modern Leadership. His research showed that the soft skills of empathy, transparency, collaboration, and flexibility—and other skills that have been traditionally viewed as feminine—are no longer nice-to-have characteristics for leaders but foundational to Modern Leadership.

You Need to Know

"Soft" Skills Are Today's Power Skills

Human resource expert, Josh Bersin, believes we need to reframe people-forward "soft" skills as the engine that drives career and company success. He calls them "power" skills and says, "Hard Skills are soft (they change all the time, are constantly being obsoleted, and are relatively easy to learn), and Soft Skills are hard (they are difficult to build, critical, and take extreme effort to obtain). . . . These "soft skills" are the most important and the "hardest" skills in business. Without them you will never be a big success."[15]

The skills needed in the workforce are going to be less about IQ and a little bit more about EQ, because if you think about it, a lot of IQ knowledge is going to be available at our fingertips through hand-held devices and the computer and technologies that we have at our disposal.

—Deborah Henretta, retired group president, Asia & Global Specialty Channel, Procter & Gamble[16]

Findings from Udemy Business's 2022 Workplace Learning Trends Report revealed that "power skills" (their words) such as flexibility, empathy, and transparency are *the* secret sauce necessary to be successful at any level within an organization, and especially for managers in a hybrid workplace.[17]

At PrismWork, we recognized that Modern Leaders needed a new set of power skills to fuel their success. So, in 2020, we brought together experts in organizational psychology, DEI, leadership development, human resources, consumer insights, and culture transformation to understand the core competencies of leaders committed to sustainable impact. We interviewed scores of leaders, conducted extensive secondary research, and soon began to see patterns: empathy, humility, accountability, resiliency, and transparency were essential power skills for Modern Leaders. But we felt something was missing—something foundational to leading diverse talent.

It all came together when we realized the missing key was inclusivity. As we mentioned earlier, given the fundamental changes in the workplace and given our work with companies and their leaders, it was clear that leveraging a wide variety of perspectives in decision-making and policies must be a core tenet of Modern Leadership. Without it, new power that benefits all stakeholders can't flourish, and the status quo is maintained.

With those insights, we developed the HEARTI® model of leadership competencies—the six power skills we identified from our research and interviews that are needed to enable Modern Leaders to use their power with intention. HEARTI stands for: humility, empathy, accountability, resiliency, transparency, and inclusivity. All six are essential for leaders who are committed to creating long-term, sustainable 3BL impact.

Humility
Aware of one's own limitations and that one's success is tied to the success of their teams/employees; focuses on the development of others.

Empathy
Understands the feelings, needs, and drivers of others; grounded in curiosity and compassion, exercises active listening.

Accountability
Delivers triple bottom-line impact; holds self and others responsible for commitments and impact of actions.

Resiliency
Perseveres and responds with agility when faced with challenges, which inspires others to continue toward purpose and impact.

Transparency
Builds trust through clear and authentic communications; has the courage to make unpopular decisions and owns one's point of view.

Inclusivity
Attracts, collaborates with, and promotes diverse talent and communities; leverages diversity to drive innovation and better business outcomes.

You Need to Know

Our Students Are the Best!

We loved it when our student Darryl Leon came up with an icon representing HEARTI using the periodic table. He began with helium (He) and argon (Ar)—both abundant noble gases—and ended with titanium (Ti) for its hard base layer and great luster. In combination, this icon represents the well-rounded, unflappable, and agile-yet-grounded Modern Leader, who capitalizes on all of the HEARTI power skills to achieve impact.

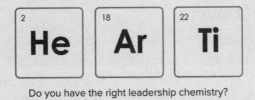

Do you have the right leadership chemistry?

The Journey Ahead

Our goal with this book, and in the work we do each and every day, is to support leaders on their journey to become as skilled, as impactful, as mission driven, and as fueled by the urgency of now as Yvon Chouinard, Indra Nooyi, Clarke Murphy, and Deepa Purushothaman. These four are just a few of the thousands—and, we hope, eventually millions—of leaders who understand that new approaches and new skills are needed to achieve our collective goal: long-term sustainable impact that drives prosperity for generations to come.

Over the next six chapters, we detail each of the core competencies of the HEARTI model.

You'll learn how other leaders have used their HEARTI power skills to deliver impact, see how HEARTI power skills connect actions to business outcomes, and gain insights into why the HEARTI model is *the* tool to help you uplevel your leadership so you can solve the urgent challenges facing our world. When you hone the six HEARTI power skills, you'll be able to use your power with intention, gain the success you deserve, and make the sustainable impact our world needs.

Now, read on!

Reframe

Traditional Leadership

Leading and/or influencing a group of people to achieve a singular outcome resulting in financial benefits for the company and its shareholders. Traditional Leaders have a high estimate of their own importance and are focused on outcomes that benefit themselves and their individual network/community. They are focused on the single bottom line.

Who Is a Traditional Leader?

Only those individuals at the senior level of an organization are designated a leader. The result of this approach to leadership is that power is centralized at the top of the organization.

Modern Leadership

Leading and/or influencing a group of people to achieve positive, long-term sustainable outcomes that result in prosperity for all stakeholders. Modern Leaders are humble, empathetic, resilient, and inclusive. They are transparent in their communications in order to build trust and are accountable to more than just their own needs and desires. Modern Leaders are focused on the triple bottom line.

Who Is a Modern Leader?

You are! Modern Leaders can be found at every level of the organization. Leadership at all levels is a paradigm, in which regardless of your title, tenure, or compensation, you engage, generate ideas, and make decisions from a place of ownership. Modern Leaders know that they can and do have influence no matter what level or department they are in the company, enabling more democratic decision-making, more decentralized power, and more collective purpose-driven impact.

Evolving Your Leadership

Where Are You on Your Journey to Becoming a Modern Leader?

We will end each chapter with practical actions you can take to evolve your leadership. Before we move on, we invite you to take a moment and ask yourself, "Where do I show up on the Modern Leadership Core Competency Continuum?" With that clarity, you can then begin to evolve your HEARTI power skills for success.

(continued)

Modern Leadership: The Core Competency Continuum

HEARTI	Unready	Evolving	Best in Class
Humility	Considers solely personal career needs: "What have I done for me?"	Considers needs of the company; "What have I done for us?"	Considers needs of all stakeholders; "What have I done for others?"
Empathy	Lacks insight into the needs and motivations of others; Defensive	Understands the needs of others; Often exhibits rescuing behavior	Prioritizes the development of others; Empowers cultures of curiosity and learning
Accountability	Ignores impact of cross-team interdependencies; Sets unclear objectives and measurements; Inconsistent decision-making	May be inconsistent in holding self and others accountable	Leads clear accountability and responsibility; Holds self and others accountable to purpose-driven decision-making; Willing to take a stand
Resiliency	Follower, unwilling to innovate; Comfort with the familiar; Personalized company failures	Reactive to business realities; Can separate company failures from personal shortcomings	Able to adapt through agile response to challenges and failures. Understands the challenges that accompany inclusive leadership
Transparency	Reactive and hoards information as a way to manage and maintain power; Afraid to take a stand	Responsive and increases knowledge sharing with reporting and metrics; Improved communications and more frequent meetings / check-ins	Proactive and committed to ongoing communication with public reporting on key metrics including DE&I and pay equity; Committed to taking an uncomfortable stand; Thought leader
Inclusivity	Scarcity-driven; Unconscious bias; Resistant to sharing privilege; No tracking of data; Fiefdoms and ingroups	Awareness of DE&I, but lacking individual and team accountability; "Nice to have" but not connected to bottom line	Delivers a world of belonging; Diversity and inclusion is built into the DNA of the company

3

Be Humble: "Lead from Behind"

ADVERTISING CEO Ian Sohn wasn't looking to get on national television, be covered in international news, or have his social media post go viral reaching millions of people around the world. But that's what happened in May 2019 when he wrote a treatise to his employees on LinkedIn.

Here's the backstory: Ian's a single dad who co-parents with his ex-wife. He'd been traveling nonstop for over three weeks and was finally home for one weekend before he was supposed to head out on yet another business trip. It was Saturday morning, and he was looking forward to an excursion with his two boys when he received an email from a colleague asking if he could "just grab a quick call" to discuss a client issue. Ian spent over an hour composing a response for why he couldn't talk that day. Then, Ian had an epiphany. He didn't want to have to apologize for having a life and didn't want his employees to feel that way either. So Ian emailed his coworker, "You know what, Bill? I'll talk to you on Monday." The response? "Great, fine. Talk to you on Monday. No big deal."

Later that day, Ian wrote his now famous LinkedIn post broadcasting his leadership philosophy, which he summarizes as, "You don't need to explain yourself to me. If you are accountable to your teams and to your clients, and you get the job done. I don't care how you do it, where you do it, or when you do it. As a boss, my vow to you is: I will never treat you like a child. I will do my best to help you do your best work. How you do it is up to you."

In his viral LinkedIn post, Ian wrote:

> "I deeply resent how we've infantilized the workplace. How we feel we have to apologize for having lives. That we don't trust adults to make the right decisions. How constant connectivity/availability (or even the perception of it) has become a valued skill.
>
> I'm equally grateful for the trust/respect my peers, bosses and teams show me every day.
>
> Years ago, a very senior colleague reacted with incredulity that I couldn't fly on 12 hours notice because I had my kids that night. I didn't feel the least bit guilty, which I could tell really bothered said colleague. But it still felt horrible.
>
> I never want you to feel horrible for being a human being."

Ian's message about treating his employees as adults touched a nerve. He suddenly found himself trending on social media and was asked by major news outlets to discuss his view on Modern Leadership. A reporter on CNBC asked Ian, "As a boss, don't you want to know where your employees are in the middle of the day and they're not at their desk?" He responded, "I hire good people with high integrity and trust them to do a good job, and they do. I am not interested in micro-managing them. It's not *my* job as their leader."[1]

In the fall of 2020, when Ian first visited our Stanford class as a guest executive, he told our students, "I never expected to become famous for telling people I respect them as humans, and frankly, I shouldn't be. This is not fake humility. I spoke up because I wanted to send a message to other leaders to encourage them to be better. What used to work as a leader doesn't anymore. The truth is every leader should be sending this message."

In his autobiography, *Long Walk to Freedom*, Nelson Mandela[2] argued great leaders "lead from behind" much like a shepherd who "stays behind the flock, letting the most nimble go out ahead, whereupon the others follow, not realizing that all along they are being directed from behind." This "in-service" style of leadership was tested globally during the pandemic. Sadly, many leaders failed.

In May 2021, as Covid appeared to be waning and vaccines were proliferating, CEOs began insisting their employees return to the office, claiming it was better for "productivity," "culture," and "teamwork." Their arguments flew in the face of facts as employees resoundingly reported preferring the freedom to work from anywhere and as productivity spikes were seen in the vast majority of industries around the globe. In fact, in the midst of Covid the world's output per hour worked surged by 4.9%, more than double the long-term average annual rate of 2.4% registered between 2005 and 2019. This is the fastest global growth in hourly productivity observed since data have been available.[3] Meanwhile, profits at many companies also surged. In late 2020 and early 2021, many global companies saw unprecedented profit spikes. For example, as the majority of JPMorgan Chase's 240,000 global employees worked from home during this time, the bank saw its Q1 2021 profits increase by 399%. But by spring of 2021, that didn't stop CEO Jamie Dimon from insisting the company's employees return to the office.

At an industry conference, Jamie announced, "We want people back to work, . . . and yes, the commute, you know people don't like commuting, but that's life. So what." He went on to say, "Work from home doesn't work for those who want to hustle."[4]

Like Ian before him, Jamie's comments went viral; within days "hustle culture" became a meme. But unlike Ian, Jamie was lambasted for his lack of empathy and, more importantly, his lack of humility. His "my way or the highway," inflexible approach is a classic example of Traditional Leadership, the kind that the US Army has declared ineffective and, worse, high risk.

As we mentioned in the previous chapter, after decades of insisting on top-down, authoritarian leadership, the US Army released a 62-page report in 2019 revamping its philosophy of best-in-class leadership. Core to it all: humility.[5]

"The most effective leaders . . . possess the humility to ask themselves hard questions about their performance, decisions, and judgment."

Humility . . . is a sign of a leader being unselfish, working toward something more important than themselves.

—US Army on Leadership, 2019

The report goes on to detail counterproductive and high-risk leadership behaviors "that result from self-centered motivations on the part of the leader, where they act in ways that seek primarily to accomplish their own goals and needs before those of others. Specific examples include, but are not limited to, displaying arrogance, lacking concern or empathy for others, taking credit for others' work, insisting on having their way, distorting information to favor their own ideas, exaggerating accomplishments or abilities, putting own work and accomplishments ahead of others' and the mission, displaying narcissistic tendencies, or exhibiting a sense of entitlement."

Leadership today, according to the Army, must end the hierarchical concept of "leader's rule" where those below said leader must follow commands without question. Modern Leadership follows the concept of "leader's intent" where underlings are seen as colleagues and teammates who are empowered to make their own decisions to meet the collective goal.

In other words, according to the US Army, Modern Leaders must take a "we" approach—and it all starts with humility.

The Essence of Humble Leadership

We live in such chaotic uncertain times and there is no play-book to tell us what the right decision or action is . . . which means we need to have a very healthy dose of humility so we can learn from one another, learn from our mistakes, and realize that as a leader we are not going to have all of the answers or skills or experiences to get us through.

—Eric Dube, CEO of Travere Therapeutics

In her TED Talk on the lessons we can learn from presidents, historian Doris Kearns Goodwin said of Abraham Lincoln,

"He possessed an uncanny ability to empathize with and think about other people's point of view. He repaired injured feelings that might have escalated into permanent hostility. He shared credit with ease. He assumed responsibility for the failure of his subordinates. He constantly acknowledged his errors and learned from his mistakes. He refused to be provoked by petty grievances. He never submitted to jealousy or brooded over perceived slights."

Lincoln's mission was to heal a divided country and, Kearns Goodwin argues, it was his humility that was the secret to success. In Modern Leadership terms, we'd say Lincoln demonstrated a "growth mindset"—the fundamental belief that a person's capabilities and talents can be improved with effort and insight. Leaders who exhibit a growth mindset seek out new ideas and test their assumptions. In doing so, they expand their capabilities and impact.

In Lincoln's case, his growth mindset meant he was not threatened by his "team of rivals" but rather was challenged to think differently and to find solutions he may not have imagined on his own.[6]

Much like Lincoln, Modern Leaders:

- Have an awareness of their own limitations;
- Understand that their success is tied to the success of their teams/employees;
- Operate with a service mindset;
- Are open to new ideas and contradictory information;
- Are driven by a higher purpose beyond the self.

It isn't always easy, but these characteristics can be learned. Sandy Macrae, CEO of Sangamo Therapeutics, knows this only too well. In 2020, his chief people officer, Whitney Jones, hired our company, PrismWork, to help Sangamo leverage the opportunity brought about by the pandemic to revisit and strengthen their corporate culture. Despite the lockdown, many Sangamo employees continued to work on-site in offices and laboratories, while others had shifted to work from home. Sangamo saw the advantage of emphasizing a #bettertogether culture not only for the physical return to office, but also to increase engagement across the global team.

We surveyed Sangamo's employees and conducted numerous focus groups to understand their experiences. The resounding message was that work-from-anywhere was helping Sangamo's employees be productive, have control of their schedules, and ensure the safety and well-being of their families. They weren't arguing for a permanent work-from-anywhere policy, just more flexibility, at least for now.

We spoke to the leadership team to understand their motivation for the culture refresh and the impact on work locations. As Sandy shared, "I like the energy I get from those chance hallway encounters, the buzz of activity as our teams collaborate and ideate together. It's how we build our culture. And, truth be known, as a leader, it's what I am most familiar with."

It takes courage to break beyond the familiar. But unlike so many other leaders, Sandy Macrae proved himself a Modern

Leader by listening to his employees, responding with humility, and collaborating to find solutions that worked for all.

We worked with Sandy, Whitney, and the rest of the leadership team to use this unprecedented moment to revamp their culture. Together, we updated their values, provided leadership workshops, and mapped out how they could revise their global programs and policies to be more responsive to the realities of the modern workplace and talent needs. Today, despite ongoing challenges in the business environment, continued chaos from the pandemic, employees at Sangamo report they "know the company has their back," and that has helped drive loyalty and engagement.

As Sandy told us, "I came of age in a time when leaders were able to dictate what their employees did, but I realized that was not going to get the results we wanted. Our success depends on our employees' ownership of the mission and strategy and then empowering them to do their best work in the way that works best for them and their teams. I learned so much from challenging my own biases. By listening to our employees and making decisions based on those responses, we delivered a better outcome for all."

Ian Sohn and Sandy Macrae may have been raised in the era of Traditional Leadership, but with humility they were able to adapt to what is needed today and were able to increase their influence, power, and impact.

Humility: Better for Business?

It's hard to argue that humility is the better business strategy when leaders such as Elon Musk are seemingly so effective in their utter lack of humility. But the exception should not be confused with the rule.

Sure, Elon Musk and Mark Zuckerberg have made lots of money for themselves and their investors in the process. But are they the paragons of Modern Leadership? Are their actions and choices better for the entirety of stakeholders? Do their behaviors and decisions lead to sustainable outcomes for the company, the employees, the world at large? We argue, "No!" But there isn't much research linking humility and long-term business outcomes to back us up.

A 2014 survey of more than 1,500 workers from Australia, China, Germany, India, Mexico, and the US focused on the following core behavioral attributes:

- Learning from criticism and admitting mistakes;
- Empowering followers to learn and develop;
- Acts of courage, such as taking personal risks for the greater good;
- Holding employees responsible for results.[7]

In assessing managers who exhibited these traits, the study found that their employees were more likely to report feeling included in their workgroups. In other words, humble leadership resulted in an increased sense of belonging, and this was true for both women and men. As a result, they were more likely to engage in team behavior, go beyond the call of duty, and pick up the slack for an absent colleague.

And, importantly, the study revealed that employees of humble leaders reported being more innovative, more comfortable suggesting new product ideas, and more willing to recommend ways of doing work better. Attitudes and approaches that undoubtedly drive better bottom-line results.

Another study conducted in 2015 of 105 small to mid-sized tech companies revealed that humble chief executives are more likely than others to have upper-management teams that collaborate, share information, jointly make decisions, and possess a shared vision. Senior leadership alignment built on humility led to greater company-wide efficiency, innovation, and profitability. An unexpected outcome of the study was the impact of humility on pay equity. Those companies with a more humble leader also tended to have lower pay disparity between the

CEO and the management team, although the link to pay equity among all employees was not assessed.[8]

We're confident time will show that humble leadership is key to attracting and retaining great employees, delivers more innovative solutions, and results in more inclusive workplace cultures, and we look forward to seeing the proof.

> *A leader must dismantle ego and focus on contributing value to society.*
>
> **—John Gerzema, co-CEO of Harris Poll[9]**

Why Is Humility So Rare in Leadership Today?

There are three key reasons humility is such a rarity in leadership, and it has much to do with our collective misguided and old-fashioned notions of what it means to be a leader. Traditionally, we have perceived "true" leaders as confident, charismatic, and "strong" rather than humble. Below we detail how these old troupes harm Modern Leaders and why humility is a power skill.

Confidence versus Competence

> *Humility happens when you realize that you aren't half as good as you think.*
>
> **—Guy Kawasaki, marketing evangelist and author**

"Have you worked with people who are not as good as they think?" asks psychologist Dr. Tomas Chamorro-Premuzic[10] in his book *Why Do So Many Incompetent Men Become Leaders?* Tomas argues that one of the reasons so many "average" men rise to the top is our collective inability to distinguish between confidence and competence. It's an aspect of something called the Dunning-Kruger effect popularized by social psychologists David Dunning and Justin Kruger who, in 1999, published a study entitled "Unskilled and Unaware of It: How Difficulties in Recognizing One's Own Incompetence Lead to Inflated Self-Assessments."

The Dunning-Kruger effect occurs when a person's lack of knowledge and skills in a certain area cause them to overestimate their own competence. This is a type of cognitive bias, a systematic thought process caused by the tendency of the human brain to simplify information processing through a filter of personal experience and preference. In other words, a subjective reality. Repeated research has shown that most of us think we are better than the average, and many of us lack the ability to recognize . . . our lack of ability. Without self-awareness, we convince ourselves we are better at something than we are. As Dr. Chamorro-Premuzic argues, "One of the best ways to fool other people into thinking you are better than you actually are, is to fool yourself."

The Dunning-Kruger Effect

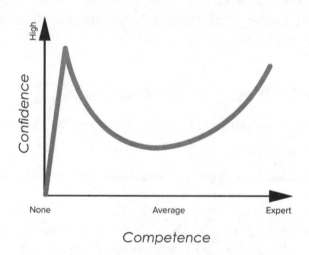

Here's the irony: the more competent an individual becomes, the more likely they are to lose confidence for a period of time. A self-aware leader comes to a point when he or she realizes there is so much more to learn. This leads to a drop in confidence until they gain more competence and expertise. Eventually, the self-aware leader builds the expertise they need to be truly good and they regain confidence, becoming a more moderate and humble leader.

One critical way to speed up the process and break beyond the Dunning-Kruger trap is to ask for feedback. As the US Army report reveals, "It is difficult to judge our own humility. One's humility is largely determined by other people."

Unfortunately, the higher someone rises in an organization, the less likely they are to get honest feedback. Teammates and direct reports are often unwilling to speak truth to those in power, so leaders become locked in a bubble of self-reinforcing reverence. The key here

> **Decentering is a critical skill for Modern Leaders. It takes deep confidence to step aside and let others shine.**

is to build your network of honest advisors. In their book *Good Guys, How Men Can Be Better Allies for Women in the Workplace*, Drs. Brad Johnson and David Smith advise leaders to "decenter" themselves. They explain, "Decentering is the intentional act of stepping out of the central role or the primary focus of attention so that other people and their perspectives can be fully seen and heard." They go on to write, "For the best feedback, it's crucial to have a diverse network of [confidants]. Ask for constructive feedback; when you are lucky enough to receive it, accept it without being defensive."[11]

Here's another irony: the Dunning-Kruger effect can also cause those who excel in a given area to think the task is simple for everyone and thereby underestimate their own relative abilities. If something comes easy to a leader who is high in humility, they might have unrealistic expectations of the skills and abilities of others in this same area. This can become a management quagmire making others feel less accomplished and may reinforce the self-doubts or insecurities of the leader's colleagues. Or a leader might set deadlines they know they could deliver on, but other members of their team can't because they lack the same relative ability in said area. This can lead to burnout and resentment.

It is incumbent upon a Modern Leader to be realistic about the skills and abilities of their team members and to work with them to help them build their skills over time. Pushing your team faster and harder because *you* have mastery of something is not good leadership—that's what tyrants do. The best strategy is to follow Lincoln's approach and staff your team with people who bring different skills so that collectively you can deliver far beyond what you could alone.

Build a team that is so talented that they kind of, slightly make you uncomfortable to be with them, because you know you are going to have to raise your game to be with them.

—**Brian Chesky, CEO, Airbnb**[12]

Leader Tool Kit

How to Help Others Step into the Spotlight

Ten things you can do to build your team's competence and confidence:

1) Understand team members' individual career goals and how the given project can support their development.

2) Have a clear idea of their individual strengths and weaknesses.

3) Be explicit and detailed about what the project needs to be completed with excellence.

4) Set realistic deadlines and adjust as needed.

5) Let them try to solve the problem on their own.

6) Offer to explain how you would approach the challenge/issue.

7) Give constructive feedback so they can learn from their mistakes and course correct as necessary.

8) Celebrate the effort all along the way.

9) Amplify the wins to others while giving credit to the team.

10) Debrief after the project is completed to discuss what went well, what could be improved upon, and what each team member learned in the process.

Charisma

Let's be clear, the guilty party here is not just the overinflated ego of the incompetent, it is society's collective fascination with leaders who are charming, entertaining, and, in many cases, narcissistic. Social media has fueled the rise of those who are famous for just being famous. Who hasn't spent hours distracting themselves with shows like *Keeping Up with the Kardashians* or scrolling through Instagram or TikTok following our favorite celebrity influencer? These charismatic personalities garner our attention and our following. But charisma is not a reliable metric of sustainable, positively impactful leadership.

Susan Cain, author of *Quiet: The Power of Introverts in a World That Can't Stop Talking,* argues that our emphasis on extroversion (read: charisma) limits the potential of over half the population who self-identify as introverts.[13] "The bias in our culture against introversion is so deep and so profound. Our most important institutions—our schools, our workplaces— are designed for extroverts."[14] She goes on to say that "despite research that shows that introverts drive better business out-comes because they are more likely to let their employees run with their ideas, introverts are routinely passed up for leadership positions."

Meanwhile, all of this pressure to be charismatic is having negative impacts on leaders. Morra Aarons-Mele, author of *The Anxious Achiever: Turn Your Biggest Fears into Your Leadership Superpower*, says "Our society's fascination with charisma is placing extreme pressure on leaders, but the truth is most of the leaders I speak to are struggling with anxiety and the pressure to be perfect all of the time. It's time for leaders to be more open and authentic about their challenges so others can see it is not as rosy as it might look on social media."

The knowledge of how little you can do alone teaches you humility.

—Eleanor Roosevelt

Arrogance

We've already discussed how confidence on its face is not a bad thing, except when it is not substantiated by competence. Mean-while, arrogance is often confused with confidence. Arrogance is defined as behaving as if you are more important, or know more, than other people. Arrogant people are driven by low self-esteem and competition. Confidence is grounded in experi-ence and expertise with a sense of respect and humility; whereas arrogance is grounded in baseless confidence that lacks respect for the contribution and capabilities of others. This can be espe-cially true when it comes to Modern Leadership.

In 2021, PrismWork partnered with nFormation and the Billie Jean King Leadership Initiative to gain a clear understanding of the experiences of women of color in the knowledge workspace. Our research, PowHER Redefined,[15] revealed many insights including a glaring reality that some high-performing leaders were also bullies whose toxic behavior directly impacted the careers of women of color. These "toxic rock stars," as we called them, delivered results for the company but in the process created cultures that were much more likely to be racist, sexist, and homophobic. One consistent description we heard about these individuals was that they were "arrogant."

Companies with a short-term focus on profits are often loath to fire toxic rock stars. At one of our client companies, turnover in the sales division was as high as 48%. The reason? A head of sales who delivered the numbers but who was killing the very culture the new CEO was trying to establish. As the CEO explained, "I know he's a problem, but he delivers the results our shareholders want to see. How can I fire him when we have revenue goals we need to meet?"

But the impact of continuing to reward these arrogant high performers on company culture, and on diverse talent in particular, has huge ramifications. Research has shown that toxic cultures cost US companies almost $50 billion per year,[16] and toxic culture was the single biggest predictor of attrition during the first six months of the Great Resignation.[17]

> It's past time for company leaders to stop rewarding arrogance and to start rewarding humble leaders who are culturally competent.

A woman of color who was previously a senior partner at a global consulting agency said to us after she had left the company, "Enough is enough. Toxic rock stars are a cancer on company culture. Leaving them in a position of power reveals what the company truly values: profits over people."

While companies struggle to get this right, so do individuals. It's important to understand that humility exists on a continuum. Leaders who lack humility can show up as arrogant and overconfident and can be at risk for making rash decisions that don't take into account the experiences or expertise of others.

But too much humility can be misconstrued as being weak or lacking in authority. The US Army report makes this clear:

> "Too little humility represents arrogance or hubris, which may lead to overconfidence. Excess humility is problematic because it is interpreted as shyness, meekness, passivity, blind obedience, or timidity. Either extreme signals a lack of self-awareness that undermines followers' trust and confidence in the leader's ability to make good decisions, look out for the unit's welfare, and to achieve success."[18]

As a result, a Modern Leader must operate with self-awareness. It takes humility and courage to gain true self-awareness. According to organizational psychologist Tasha Eurich[19], while 95% of people *think* they are self-aware, only 10–15% truly are. In her book *Insight: The Power of Self-Awareness in a Self-Deluded World,* she explains that true self-awareness is the ability to see ourselves clearly—to understand who we are, how others see us, and how we fit into the world. But don't spend too much time obsessing about yourself. That's not humble.

True humility is not thinking less of yourself, it is thinking of yourself less.

—C. S. Lewis

Modern Leaders recognize that humility is a power skill that is foundational for their success. They know the best leaders are those who are focused on service—service to their employees, service to their clients and/or customers, and service to the world at large.

Reframe

Humility Is a Power Skill

- Increases your influence and impact;
- Drives deeper employee engagement and loyalty;
- Encourages more innovative solutions;
- Promotes a growth mindset;
- Focuses teams on the collective mission;
- Can result in more equitable workplace programs and policies (e.g. pay equity);
- Delivers better bottom-line results.

Evolving Your Leadership

Ten Ways to Increase Your Humility

1) Get clarity: Be aware of your own strengths and weaknesses by seeking honest feedback.

2) Develop a growth mindset: Be committed to learning and evolving.

3) Seek to understand: Ask what others need … and listen.

4) Serve: Help others to grow and develop.

5) Delegate: Let go of perfectionism and micromanagement.

6) Deliver with competence: Build your skills and deliver what you—and your team—commit to with excellence.

7) Collaborate: Have a team-first mindset.

8) Focus on results: Communicate your leader's intent oriented around outcomes, not actions.

9) Own it: Apologize when you are wrong or have made a mistake.

10) Amplify: Share the spotlight.

4

Be Empathetic: It's Not How You Feel, It's What You Do

MARIA ROSS, author of *Empathy Edge: Harnessing the Value of Compassion as an Engine for Success*, is an expert on the power of empathy in the workplace. She is also a regular guest executive to our class. According to Maria, "Empathy is *the* engine for business results in today's complex world." But, as she explains to our students, our capacity for empathy is under attack as never before.

"When it comes to empathy, each and every one of us has been tested these past few years," Maria told our students in the winter of 2023. "Yes. Of course. Covid. But our empathy was being already challenged well before the global pandemic pushed us to the brink."

She's right. Let's start with the onslaught of natural disasters that have been piling up including hurricanes, earthquakes, floods, tornadoes, wildfires, and on and on and on. Add to that news of refugees fleeing chaos from around the globe, reports of alleged war crimes, the political upheavals and deepening distrust within the United States and beyond, the public display of violent murders of Black men and women by police, the seemingly never ending sexual harassment in the workplace, and, yes, Covid. As Maria says, "It's enough to make any leader want to dig their head in the sand and tell employees to focus on work."

That's exactly what Google CEO, Sundar Pichai, said to his employees at a January 2023 company all-hands meeting. He told them, "We should think about how we can minimize distractions and really raise the bar on both product excellence and productivity."[1]

"A total miscue," according to Maria, "and a recipe for failure." Rather than push employees to work harder, Maria argues we need to support employees to work smarter, which means in a way that supports their emotional and physical well-being. "In the midst of all of these challenges, it is more important than ever for leaders to balance the needs of the business while also bringing empathy to the workplace. The two are not mutually exclusive."

> *Empathy is the most important instrument in a leader's tool box.*
>
> **—Simon Sinek, leadership expert and author of**
> ***It Starts with Why: How Great Leaders***
> ***Inspire Everyone to Take Action***[2]

The Business Case for Empathy

As we explained in Chapter 2, for decades soft leadership skills such as empathy have gotten short shrift relative to hard skills such as financial acumen, which can be measured and quantified. But companies and their leaders are beginning to recognize the link between empathy and the triple bottom line.

> *The value that I really learned to appreciate deeply and which I talk about a great deal is empathy. I don't see it as simply a "nice to have" but I believe it is at the center of the agenda for innovation.*
>
> **—Satya Nadella, CEO of Microsoft**[3]

When it comes to empathy, here are some of the few ways it delivers better business outcomes.

Higher Employee Engagement

It's been shown that engaged employees are more productive, experience less burnout, and are less likely to leave an organization.[4] But how do you engage your employees? The answer? Empathy. A 2021 study by Catalyst revealed that 76% of workers who experienced empathy from their senior management reported feeling engaged at work, compared to the 32% of workers who felt their management was not empathetic.[5]

Higher Productivity

Want to increase your employees' output? Be more empathetic. A recent study on "quiet quitting" found that those managers who are seen by their employees as most able to "balance getting results with a concern for others' needs" saw 62% of their direct reports willing to give extra effort versus the 20% of direct reports working with the least effective managers who said they'd go the extra mile.[6]

Increased Innovation

Innovation is key to a company's ability to stay ahead of the competition, so anything that helps increase innovation should be a priority for a leader. What drives innovation? Empathy. That Catalyst study referenced earlier also revealed that 61% of employees who had an empathic leader viewed themselves as being more creative and innovative compared to just 13% of employees with less-empathetic bosses.[7] Global consulting firm McKinsey argues that fostering a culture of trust where employees feel a sense of psychological safety is key to driving innovation.[8] Modern Leaders foster cultures of trust by bringing empathy (more on psychological safety and empathy later).

Improved Retention

Modern Leaders know that hiring great employees is one thing but retaining them, another. The goal is, of course, to keep your best talent. How do you do that? Empathy. According to Business Solver's 2021 *State of Workplace Empathy* study, 93% of employees reported they would stay with an empathetic employer, and 82% of employees would leave their position to work for a more empathetic organization.[9] Additionally, empathy has been shown as a key retention tool for diverse talent. One study revealed that 57% of white women who feel their life circumstances are respected and valued by their company report never or rarely thinking of leaving their organization, compared to 14% of white women who do not feel valued and respected. For women of color, that same study showed those who feel their life circumstances are respected and valued by their company are 1.4 times less likely to consider leaving versus those women of color who do not feel valued and respected.[10]

Reduced Employee Burnout

Employee burnout and its impact on mental health has become a crisis in the workplace, but that's not new news. In fact, research as far back as 2003 has shown that depression alone cost US employers up to $44 billion annually in lost productivity.[11] Today, according to Businessolver, 41% of American employees are struggling with mental health and/or substance abuse. Meanwhile, an overwhelming majority (95%) of employees believe that organizations that offer mental health benefits are more empathetic than those that do not. But only 29% of employees say they're aware of their organization having an employee assistance program that offers supportive, diagnostic, referral, and counseling treatment services.[12] While research providing a direct link between reduced employee burnout and empathy has yet to have been proven, the link between burnout and *decrease*d empathy has long been understood.[13]

Modern Leaders must place mental health as central to their principles—for themselves, for their employees, for their companies, and for the world at large.

Improved ROI

Can empathy really be linked to financial metrics? The research says yes. Global consulting firm DDI developed a "Global Empathy Index," ranking 160 businesses in terms of empathy. Those companies that ranked in the top 10% as most empathetic generated 50% more income than those that ranked in the bottom 10%.[14] But why rely on stats? Consider Microsoft CEO Satya Nadella. He says embracing empathy as a core business driver has been key to enabling Microsoft's seven-fold increase in market capitalization since he took office.[15]

In his book, *Hit Refresh: The Quest to Discover Microsoft's Soul and Imagine a Better Future for Everyone,* Satya argues that without empathy, Microsoft would never succeed in understanding customer needs and delivering solutions to meet those needs. In fact, he says by putting empathy front and center, Microsoft's employees found ways to upgrade and enhance products giving customers solutions they didn't even know they needed. The result? More customer commitment to the company's products and services, which means more money to the bottom line.[16]

Why Empathy Matters for Modern Leaders

The power of empathy is not just what it does for the company, it's also about what it does for a Modern Leader's career.

Increases Ethical Decision-Making

Ethics and how to make decisions around those ethics is key for all Modern Leaders committed to triple bottom-line impact. Research has shown that ethical decision-making is rooted in empathy. A 2022 study of emergency room nurses facing the Covid pandemic in China proved that those who ranked high in empathy were significantly more likely to make ethical decisions when it came to patient care.[17] A meta-analysis of college students linked empathy to increased commitments to social justice,[18] and other research has shown the link between empathy and prosocial behaviors.[19] In brief, being empathetic may be essential to broadening the focus from short-term shareholder capitalism to the wider, more impactful lens of stakeholder capitalism.

Reduces Burnout

As noted earlier, the link between leaders who exhibit empathy and reduced employee burnout has yet to be definitively proven, but there is ample research that being empathetic can reduce a leader's own experience of burnout. One study of police officers showed a significant association between empathy and burnout: officers with higher dispositional empathy actually had *lower* levels of burnout.[20] Additionally, studies of health care workers have shown that empathy reduces burnout.[21] Modern Leaders know that having empathy for themselves is key to being able to show up for others.

Enables Leaders to Be More Emotionally Connected and Authentic

The thing about empathy is that it doesn't just enable others to feel seen, heard, and supported, it enables Modern Leaders to be seen, heard, and supported as well. Why? Because to be empathetic requires leaders to be vulnerable and vice versa. It also requires a leader to be more connected to their own emotions and that means being vulnerable, even if it is only to one's self. Brene Brown says, "Empathy is not automatic, it is a choice and it is a vulnerable choice. In order to connect with you, I have to connect with something in myself that knows that feeling."[22]

Without vulnerability we can't access our own experiences that allow us to be empathic, and we also can't share important personal moments so that others can relate to us. Empathy is fuel for Modern Leaders to be more wholehearted and authentic.

> *The privilege of a lifetime is being who you are.*
>
> **—Joseph Campbell**

Enhances Promotability

A study from the Center for Creative Leadership of 6,731 managers from 38 countries found that leaders who viewed their managers as more empathetic to their direct reports were seen as higher performers and were more likely to promote those managers.[23]

So want to be on the fast track? Up your empathy.

Empathy Is More Than a Feeling

The dictionary defines empathy as the ability to understand and share the feelings of others. It means you're aware of another person's feelings and the impact those feelings have on that person's perceptions of their experiences. It doesn't mean you agree with how they see things; rather, being empathetic means being willing and able to appreciate what someone else is going through and, when appropriate, to support them to find solutions that work for them.

Empathetic leaders take the time to try and understand what another person (stakeholder) might be feeling or experiencing, while having the humility to recognize they can never truly understand the feelings or experiences of another. The goal of an empathetic leader is to act in a way that communicates their empathetic support and understanding of stakeholders' needs and experiences.

But empathy is far more than about feelings alone, it's about impact and action. Empathy for a Modern Leader means acknowledging the other person's feelings and take action to support them. How *you feel* is one thing; how others *experience you through your actions* is another. Modern Leaders understand this nuance.

In our HEARTI 360° research, we have found many leaders who tell us they feel great empathy for their employees and colleagues and, as a result, score themselves high in empathy. But when we ask the colleagues of said leader if she or he is empathetic and how it shows up for them, there is not always alignment.

For example, we had one leader of a global company who scored himself incredibly high on empathy. He told us he felt deeply about the challenges his employees were going through in the midst of Covid, particularly those employees who were parents. But his employees scored him very low on empathy. "His intentions are good. He says all the right things, but when it comes down to it, he hasn't *done* anything to reduce burnout or to make our lives easier," one of his direct reports told us.

As Michael Brenner, author of *Mean People Suck: How Empathy Leads to Bigger Profits and a Better Life*, says, "Empathy is all about action—you don't show empathy through what you say, but what you do."[24]

The Three Types of Empathy

Given its link to business outcomes, there is little doubt that empathy is a critical skill for leaders, but empathy is far more complex than you might think. It turns out there are three types of empathy: cognitive (head/thinking), emotional (heart/feeling), and compassionate (hands/doing). Understanding this nuance is key to being a Modern Leader so you can appropriately take action.

Three Types of Empathy

Cognitive	(Head/Thinking)	Perspective taking on an intellectual level
Emotional	(Heart/Feeling)	Physically feeling what someone else is feeling
Compassionate	(Hands/Doing)	Feeling with someone and taking supportive action (if needed)

Cognitive Empathy

In cognitive empathy, one uses their intellect to identify the emotion another person is experiencing. It is perspective taking on an intellectual level. Recognizing emotions is at the core of cognitive empathy; it is being able to put yourself into someone else's place and see things from their perspective. It helps you understand another's experience. Social psychologists Sara Hodges and Michael Myers define cognitive empathy as "having more complete and accurate knowledge about the contents of another person's mind, including how the person feels." They argue cognitive empathy is a skill: Humans learn to recognize and understand others' emotional state as a way to process emotions and behavior. They argue this can be taught.[25] For example, people on the autism spectrum often struggle with cognitive empathy,[26] and more tools are created each year to help them match facial and body expression to emotions.

Emotional Empathy

Emotional empathy is when you quite literally feel the other person's emotions with them, as if you had "caught" the emotions. You may have seen another person's distress and feel emotions welling up inside your own body. Emotional empathy has also been called affective empathy and can be described as physically experiencing another's emotions. For example, you start crying because a dear friend or colleague is crying or you become angry because your coworker is enraged by how she is being treated. The challenge with emotional empathy for leaders is to not become swept up in the emotions of others. It's not easy, but learning the skill of creating healthy boundaries is key to managing emotional empathy.

You Need to Know

Emotional Empathy Is . . .

Good because it means we can readily understand and feel other people's emotions. Not only can we put ourselves in another's shoes, we can understand how it feels to be in their situation.

Bad because it is possible to become overwhelmed by those emotions and therefore be unable to respond. This is known as *empathy overload*. Those with a tendency to become overwhelmed need to work on their self-regulation and particularly their self-control so they become better able to manage their own emotions.

Compassionate Empathy

Compassionate empathy is feeling someone's pain, and offering support. This is the heart of allyship and core for Modern

Leaders. We can identify and feel another person's emotion as if it was happening to us and therefore express the appropriate amount of sympathy or congratulations. At the same time, we can also remain in control of our own emotions and apply reason to the situation. This means we can make better decisions and provide appropriate support to the individual when and where it is necessary.

How do we find a balance? If cognitive empathy is under-emotional and emotional empathy, by contrast, is perceived as overly emotional, exercising compassionate empathy is that place where we might be able to find, perhaps, a healthy balance or a reasonable balance between logic and emotion. It is vital to be clear that their experience is not your experience. For Modern Leaders, compassionate empathy is the right balance between recognizing someone's emotions, having healthy boundaries so those emotions don't overwhelm you, and then working together to find the appropriate support.

Leader Tool Kit

How to Support a Colleague with Compassionate Empathy

It starts with asking prompting/validating questions, listening for your colleague's response, be clear for yourself that the other's experience is not your experience by creating emotional space between their reality and yours, and then partnering with them to determine the best course of action:

1) "Let me see if I understand you correctly. First, you said ... Second, you said ... Do I have that right?" *Pause and listen* Follow up with, "How would you like me to support you?"

(continued)

2) "If I heard you correctly, it sounds like you are feeling . . ." *Pause and listen* Follow up with, "How would you like me to support you?"

3) "It sounds like you are dealing with a lot right now. In this moment, do you want me to take action or would you rather I listen for a while before we look for solutions?"

A student in our class shared a personal example of compassionate empathy. He told us the following story:

"Yesterday, I got a call from my father saying that my mother had fainted and tests had to be done. I could hear in his voice he was panicked. My first instinct was to panic as well. Then I thought about what we learned about compassionate empathy. So I stepped back, took a breath, and reminded myself that his emotion did not have to be my emotion. I told him I could hear how worried he was and that I was worried too. He calmed down and we began talking about solutions. We agreed we needed to get the tests done, and we'd wait for the results. I saw how it helps to dial down one's own emotional reactive responses. I learned that having more balance is of much better use to the other person in a difficult situation."

One last thing on definitions: It should also be noted that there is an important difference between empathy and sympathy. Put simply, empathy is our ability to understand how someone feels while sympathy is an expression of sorrow for another's situation. As Maria Ross explains it, "Empathy allows you to walk alongside someone. It builds intimacy and connection. Sympathy, which is about pity, creates distance between you and the other person." The goal of a Modern Leader is to build connection, so expressing empathy, rather than sympathy, is the path to take.

Why Is Empathy So Hard in the Workplace (and What You Can Do About It)

There is a reason that empathy has not been center stage as a core competency for leadership: It means focusing on the HOW of business—the behaviors and attitudes of people and how that impacts culture—not just the WHAT—the numbers and deliverables that can be quantified and relatively easily measured. Bringing empathy to the workplace is multidimensional—and takes work. Here are seven reasons why we see leaders avoiding empathy in the workplace:

1) Empathy Takes Time

If you, like us, spend your days running from Zoom meeting to Zoom meeting or flying from one client event to another, you may not feel you have the time to slow down and engage. In fast-paced work environments, you can't just focus on the work that needs to get done. As a Modern Leader, you have to slow down, ask open-ended questions, and wait and listen with the goal of understanding what the other person is feeling and experiencing.

The good news is it really isn't that hard. In her book *Social Chemistry*, Marissa King reports that managers who simply said good morning and good evening to their employees when they joined a meeting or thanks for joining as they closed up a meeting were rated 37% more empathetic and 24% more likable.[27]

One of the companies we work with has been struggling with their culture. After interviewing a number of the executives and employees, we learned that while the leaders claimed they wanted an empathetic, inclusive culture, they were modeling a transactional culture. Managers entered Zoom calls late, rushed to get to the agenda, and ended these meetings with a to-do list for others. This happened again and again, day after day. Why? Because the leaders sent the message "We need to work harder to achieve results," which meant managers felt pressured to focus on execution and rushed in their day-to-day. The net result was employees weren't feeling appreciated, understood, or cared for by their managers. Their engagement was slipping, and resentment was building, especially among the diverse talent in the lower rungs of the organization. We coached a group of their managers on how to foster empathetic, inclusive meetings. We explained that taking the time to be fully present and to listen is key to building rapport and connection. By doing this, we explained, you'll increase engagement. Not immediately but over time. One of the happy outcomes has been hearing from the managers that they feel more connected to their teams.

2) Empathy Requires Listening

At a virtual summit hosted by PrismWork in January 2023, Clarke Murphy, the former CEO of Russell Reynolds, one of the world's premier executive recruiting firms, told the audience of hundreds of executives that one skill he saw again and again in the very best leaders was "ferocious listening."

He explained, "They have an ability to be fully present and fully absorbed in the conversation they are having with you. The result is not only do you feel heard and seen, but they learn much more than they might have if they weren't fully engaged."

We have two ears and one mouth and we should use them proportionally.

—Susan Cain, author of *Quiet: The Power of Introverts in a World That Can't Stop Talking*

To increase their empathy, every Modern Leader must slow down and listen.

In Chapter 3, "Be Humble," we talked about the power and importance of decentering yourself. Listening requires a Modern Leader to be able to truly decenter themselves and hear what the other person is saying. It means not being defensive or impatient or distracted or "the expert." It means bringing humility and empathy.

Leader Tool Kit

How to Increase Your Listening Skills

Most of us listen to speak rather than listen to understand. We are busy preparing what we are going to say next rather than hearing what the other person is trying to communicate. Listening to speak is "me" focused.

Listening to understand—also called active listening— is a way to improve mutual understanding and connection. Listening to understand is "we" focused.

When you are listening to understand:

- You set aside distractions and give the other person your full attention.

- You are attentive to the speaker's posture, emotion, and level of energy.

- You hear what the person is saying and listen for what's left unsaid.

- When they are done, you repeat/summarize what they said and ask if that is what they meant and/or accurate.

- You pause to fully listen to their response.

- You ask open-ended questions such as "And what else?" or "And how did you feel about that?" to dig deeper and see if there is something more that they need or want to communicate.

Adapted from the Core Principles of Active Listening, United States Institute of Peace.[28]

3) Empathy Requires a Growth Mindset

There is research that there is actually a genetic component to empathy. Turns out that some people have a gene that triggers greater sensitivity to the hormone oxytocin. When we feel connected to people, oxytocin floods our neural pathways. For those who are genetically more sensitive to oxytocin, they are more likely to respond and engage empathetically. Additionally, recent research conducted on hundreds of thousands of women and men around the world has shown that women are better at cognitive empathy.[29] Other research has shown that in response to a baby's cry, men tend to release more stress hormones but are less likely to behave empathetically.[30] Is it nature? Is it nurture? The research is unclear. But nature or nurture, the research is definitive: you can always increase your empathy.[31]

4) Empathy Means Letting Go

Leaders are trained to be problem solvers, and yes, compassionate empathy—the goal of a Modern Leader—is ultimately about taking action. But it is not about solving the problems of others, it is about empowering them to solve it for themselves.

As you'll see in Chapter 5, "Be Accountable," empathy and accountability are directly related. To be truly effective, Modern Leaders must be both empathetic *and* accountable, but sometimes using these critical Modern Leader skills concurrently can be a challenge.

How does this show up? For starters, empathy can be overused and result in rescuing behaviors. What do we mean by rescuing behaviors? Well, for example, if a leader has an employee who's really struggling, and as a result, the leader is constantly picking up the slack, this "rescuing" of the employee can actually undermine them by not enabling them to build the skills they need to improve. Rescuing sends the message to the employee that they don't have the skills, capabilities, or authority to do the work. Rescuing can also impact the struggling employee's reputation at the company as colleagues might be misled to believe the individual isn't capable or competent. Modern Leaders let their employees learn by making mistakes, support them as they evolve, and celebrate them as they increase in skill.

5) Empathy Can Be Uncomfortable

Many Modern Leaders who are already highly empathetic struggle to give constructive feedback because they worry the feedback will hurt the feelings of their colleagues. As a result, they may avoid conversations that are uncomfortable because they fear being perceived as unkind. However, as Dr. Brené Brown[32] writes in her book *Dare to Lead: Brave Work. Tough Conversations. Whole Hearts.*, "Clear is kind. Unclear is unkind."

Providing constructive feedback that focuses on the actions and impact and not on the individual as a person is a critical skill for Modern Leaders—well, for all leaders. Many leaders have not been taught how to give feedback in a positive and productive way. This behavior generates undesirable consequences as noted by the *Harvard Business Review* article "Women Get 'Nicer' Feedback, and It Holds Them Back."

Sadly, there is quite a bit of research that shows that people of color, particularly Black women, don't get the honest and true feedback they need to succeed professionally.[33] As we noted in Chapter 3, "Be Humble," PrismWork, in collaboration with the Billie Jean King Leadership Initiative and nFormation, conducted a study of over 1,500 professional women across the United States. Our research revealed that women of color felt they were much less likely to receive the critical feedback they needed to advance their careers.[34]

As one white leader told us when she reviewed the research, "We convince ourselves we are being empathetic by not "criticizing" diverse talent, but in actuality it's probably because we're afraid we might be misperceived as racist or having an agenda or just being overly critical."

She's right. The key here is to understand the most empathetic thing a leader can do is to convey the feedback diverse talent needs and support them as they grow and evolve.

Leader Tool Kit

How to Use Micro-Nudges to Give Feedback

One of the best ways we have seen to give constructive feedback that is both empathetically delivered and helps reinforce the behaviors you want is E.A.R.N. It stands for **E**vent, **A**ction, **R**esults, **N**ext Steps.

The goal of E.A.R.N. is to give immediate feedback that will help shape empathetic, inclusive behavior and perspective. The key is to use E.A.R.N. often on relatively small issues—both congratulatory and corrective.

Here is a sample of how you can use E.A.R.N. to give empathetic, constructive feedback:

Scenario:

In today's hybrid team meeting, Joe interrupted and spoke over remote participants consistently. By the end of the meeting, the topics were only being discussed by team members in the room; none of the remote team members were sharing ideas. One of the team's agreements is that all team members' ideas will be solicited and heard in staff meetings. Here is how to give Joe feedback using E.A.R N.

EVENT: Our team agreement is that all member's ideas are solicited and heard before critical decisions are made. In today's staff meeting . . .

ACTION: You interrupted or spoke over remote colleagues.

RESULTS: As a result, their ideas weren't heard, and we don't know if our solution will meet the needs of all stakeholders. We will need to host a second meeting to gain agreement.

NEXT STEPS: How can you participate in a way that encourages everyone's voice to be heard? Or what can we do in the next meeting to encourage each team member's perspective to be heard?

6) Empathy Requires Modern Leaders to Challenge Their Biases

We love the story former Jamba Juice CEO James D. White shares in his book *Anti-racist Leadership: How to Transform Corporate Culture in a Race-Conscious World*. When he was a senior executive at Nestle Purina, James worked with a leader who, as he writes in his book, needed to be "more gender aware." To help this leader, James decided to send him to a women's event. He wasn't sure if this exposure therapy would work, but James hoped that perhaps experiencing what it feels like to be in the minority might build a bit of empathy. James said later in a podcast interview,

> "We had no idea what would come of this. But the long and short of this story: after one full day being one of only 10 men in a room of 500 women, he was so stressed out from just that one day's event he couldn't make it to dinner that evening."

That exposure therapy experience was so effective that James went on to bring white executives to Black MBA and Hispanic MBA conferences. As James explained,

"If you just think of yourself as a white executive being the only one at a 10,000-person Black MBA conference, when you walk into the elevator, into every room, into every meal, it's only for two or three days. But those kinds of activities give us the chance to build and create more empathy and learning and understanding. I think we all have opportunities to do more of that."[35]

To build true empathy, Modern Leaders must be willing to challenge their biases and get comfortable with being uncomfortable.

Empathy means challenging your preconceived ideas and setting aside your sense of what you think is true in order to learn what actually is true.

—Tom Kelley, Executive Portfolio Director, IDEO; and author of *Creative Confidence: Unleashing the Creative Potential Within Us All*[36]

7) Empathy Is Emotional

For far too long emotions have been deemed unacceptable at work, but to be empathetic is to acknowledge the humanity of colleagues. This means allowing them to express themselves emotionally. While it's not okay to yell at someone, yelling can be a natural expression of frustration, just as crying at work is sometimes inevitable. A Modern Leader who brings compassionate empathy to their interactions with colleagues enables them to feel safe to express their emotions and then supports them to move beyond the heightened emotional state to a place of solutions.

And it's not just about your colleagues. It's about your own emotions, too. Research has shown that how leaders handle their emotions directly impacts their subordinates' emotions, attitudes, and behaviors. This is true for both positive and negative emotions, as leaders' positive emotions often inspire positive action and mood, while angry or sad emotions similarly instigate subordinates' anger and sadness.[37] A Modern Leader not only applies compassionate empathy for their colleagues but also for themselves. They don't deny their emotions, but they also don't overuse them. Modern Leaders use emotional self-regulation—the concept of modifying emotional responses and behaviors to achieve a desirable outcome—in order to show up with compassionate empathy at work.

> *Engage your emotions at work. Your emotions and instincts are there to help you.*
>
> **—Richard Branson, founder of the Virgin Group**[38]

Empathy and Psychological Safety

One last thing we'd like you to consider is how you foster an empathetic culture at your workplace. The key here is psychological safety. You may be familiar with Project Aristotle by Google, a project launched to understand what made the most effective teams.[39] One of philosopher Aristotle's memorable messages was that the whole is greater than the sum of its parts—the project name reflects their findings.

After studying thousands of Google employees, qualitative and quantitative measures of drivers of performance were compared between the very top teams and the less effective teams, the leaders of Project Aristotle determined that the greatest predictor of team success was psychological safety. Those teams that reported feeling the greatest amount of psychological safety outperformed everybody else.

Psychological safety as defined by Google simply means employees perceive that the consequences of taking personal risks are low—an individual will not be embarrassed or punished for taking risks. What types of risk are we talking about? "If I'm my authentic self", "If I ask for help", "If I ask the 'dumb' question", "If I suggest a harebrained idea,"—you get the point. The thing to understand is that teams that score high on psychological safety are teams who bring empathy to one another. So teams that have psychological safety are able to build a lot of empathy, because people feel safe: safe to listen and safe to share. To learn more about the importance of the power of psychological safety and empathy, check out reworkwith.google.com.

Empathy is no longer a nice to have; it is foundational to being a Modern Leader.

In summary, modern empathy is compassion in action. It's a power skill for driving business impact. Empathy is a power skill that will fuel your career and enable you to build effective, inclusive teams. It takes time and requires ferocious listening skills, a growth mindset, a willingness to cede control, the courage to be uncomfortable, and the desire to challenge your biases. All of which is to say, it's not easy, but empathy is a core power skill and essential to being a Modern Leader.

Reframe

Empathy Is a Power Skill

- Results in higher employee engagement;
- Increases employee productivity;
- Improves employee creativity and innovation;
- Ensures higher employee retention;
- Supports employee well-being and mental health;
- Delivers better financial results;
- Promotes ethical decision-making;
- Reduces your burnout;
- Enhances your promotability.

Evolving Your Leadership

Five Ways to Increase Your Empathy

1) Challenge yourself.

Undertake challenging experiences that push you outside your comfort zone. Learn a new skill, for example, such as a musical instrument, sport, or foreign language. Develop a new professional skill. Practicing unfamiliar activities will humble you, and humility is a key enabler of empathy.

2) Get out of your usual environment.

Travel, especially to new places and cultures, gives you a better appreciation for the different experiences of humans on this connected earth.

3) Get feedback.

Ask for feedback about your relationship skills (e.g. listening) from family, friends, and colleagues—and then check in with them periodically to see how you're doing.

4) Read literary fiction.

Read literature that explores personal relationships and emotions. Research has shown that high engagement in a fictional story can lead to increased empathy.[40] Institutions are now using literary fiction to help doctors, lawyers, and business school students become more empathetic. For example, at the University of California Irvine, Johanna Shapiro from the Department of Family Medicine firmly believes that reading fiction results in better doctors and has led the establishment of a humanities program to train medical students.

5) Examine your biases.

We all have hidden (and sometimes not-so-hidden) biases that interfere with our ability to listen and empathize. These are often centered on visible factors such as age, race, and gender but can be based on educational level, economic background, physical size/shape, and so on. Cultivate your sense of curiosity about yourself and how your background may have shaped your empathy.

Adapted from Andrew Sobel and Jerold Panas's book *Power Questions: Build Relationships, Win New Business, and Influence, Wiley. Feb 7, 2012.*

5

Be Accountable: To Yourself, Your Company, and the World at Large

WHEN it comes to assessing leadership, invariably accountability is ranked as one of the key attributes of a successful leader. How can you rise up the ranks if you don't deliver the goods? You've got to do what you say you are going to do. Full stop. And the faster, the better because faster means more near-term profits for investors.

But when it comes to *Modern* Leadership that drives *sustainable* benefits for *all* stakeholders, faster isn't better, and being accountable to your *specific* job goals isn't enough. Widening the lens of what—and whom—you are accountable to is core to being a Modern Leader. With the right mindset and approach, accountability is an opportunity to stand in your power and live your purpose.

It's also an opportunity to build trust with key stakeholders. Business happens in an environment of trust. One of the essential ingredients for building trust is being accountable. If you don't hold yourself accountable and deliver what you've promised, then others can't trust you or their experience with you. If trust is broken, we can't do business together. This is as true for individuals as it is for companies.

Consider Black History Month celebrated in the United States in February each year, originally conceived as a political effort to foster equality by highlighting the contributions of Black Americans to the evolution of the country. In recent years, companies have used this opportunity to highlight *their* commitment to racial equality by celebrating the contributions of Black Americans. Sounds good in theory, but far too often it becomes a revenue opportunity.

In 2020, Google released an inspiring video, "The Most Searched: A Celebration of Black History Makers." But the company's 2020 employment statistics revealed that only 3.7 percent of Google employees in 2020 identified as Black, a number that hadn't moved since the company started sharing its data in 2014.[7] Google's diversity report from 2023 still showed only incremental growth of their Black US workforce and leadership.[8] In 2021, Target launched its "Black Beyond Measure" campaign to celebrate Black History Month and received blowback when it sold T-shirts that reflected Black stereotypes including T-shirts with "Eat Your Greens" and "Angry Black Female" emblazoned on the front.[9]

These are just a few of the thousands of examples of how companies—and the leaders who lead them—fail when it comes to truly walking the talk on expressed values. These failures in action lead to failures in trust. We'll dive deep into how to build trust in Chapter 7, "Be Transparent," but for now, trust us, leaders and the companies they work for have to build and sustain trust to succeed, and accountability is here to help you do just that.

You Need to Know

It's Time to Walk the Talk

- 86% of global consumers insist that CEOs must take a stand on social issues (Edelman 2021 Trust Barometer).[1]

- 76% of job seekers consider a company's workforce diversity when evaluating a company and job offers (Glassdoor, 2021).[2]

- 72% of consumers believe they can vote with their dollars and look to support brands that are good citizens (Amazon Ads, 2022).[3]

- 72% of consumers think companies overstate their sustainability effort (Harris Poll, 2022).[4]

- 65% of investors say that a company's commitment to diversity, equity, and inclusion drive their investment decisions (Bloom et al., 2021).[5]

- 57% of employees would take a job at a competitor if they felt the culture was better (Deloitte Insights, 2020).[6]

The Three S's of Accountability

Traditionally, corporate or leader accountability has not been linked to triple bottom-line impact. At PrismWork, we've expanded the definition of accountability from simply accepting responsibility for

It's not just about delivering results, it's about impact.

one's *own* actions to a more comprehensive three-way or 300% approach to accountability. We call it the **Three S's of Accountability**: accountable to yourself (self), for your team and organization (system), and to the world at large (society).

300% Accountability

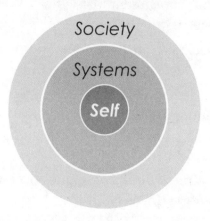

Accountability to Yourself (Self)

Jose Alvaro Avalos was 13 years old when he immigrated to the United States from Mexico with his family. He didn't speak much English, and so he was enrolled in a dual-language immersion high school program in Chicago. The summer of his junior year, Jose's dad insisted it was time his son got a job. His father did not have a college education, and as Jose told our Stanford Continuing Studies seminar, "He always wanted more for me. This is why we came to the United States, to take advantage of opportunities that were not available to us back home."

Jose worked that summer in a warehouse separating and boxing up watermelons while he sweated in the Midwestern heat. That experience convinced Jose he *had* to go to college, because, as he shared, "the alternative was not an option."

He graduated from the University of Illinois, Urbana-Champaign, with a degree in electrical engineering and was recruited into the semiconductor industry. He spent the first half of his career rising up the engineering ranks, and then Jose became an intrapreneur, starting and growing several businesses inside Intel.

When he visited our class, Jose shared an experience that illustrates the power of personal accountability and what can be learned from leaders who don't practice 300% accountability. Jose explained that when Intel shut a business down, the business unit typically paid employees' salaries for three months. During that time, the key goal is to support the employee's search for a new role *within* the company. If the employee was successful, Intel retained experienced talent, and the employee was able to maintain their paychecks and continue to provide value to the company. If no suitable role could be found, the employee left Intel and, hopefully, found an even better opportunity elsewhere. Jose saw how this strategy could go awry when he worked as a marketing director for one of Intel's divisions. He explained:

> "I remember that our executive vice president (EVP) sent out an email to everyone in the organization, and said, "Hey, we're closing the business." And then, he sent each of us a little plaque to recognize our service. At the same time, he announced that he had a "great new job as an executive at Intel." He was going to start a new business for the company while the rest of us were scrambling to find new roles. That just didn't sit well with me."

Jose did manage to find a new job within Intel and continued his climb up the company ladder. It was in 2008 when the recession hit that Jose was faced with the same challenge of his previous EVP. He explained, "Intel wanted to disinvest from the business that I was running. They came to me and said, 'Look, you need to close the business, but you don't have to worry because we have a great job for you.'"

Jose considered his options and decided he didn't want to be like his previous boss. "I said to myself, 'I don't want to be the kind of leader who redeploys all the employees, especially during a recession when there are no jobs and, at the same time, announce that I have a great new job. What kind of leader is that?!'"

Jose went to human resources and told them he wanted to remain in his current role for up to a year while he worked to find new jobs for all of the people in the division that was being closed. Reluctantly, HR agreed. Jose went on to share with our students:

> "I stayed on that job until I was able to place everybody in the organization, except for two people who found better jobs outside the company, and two people who we didn't want to retain because they were not performing at the level that we wanted them to.
>
> Staying in that role and ensuring everyone had a place to be, doing that was so rewarding to me as a person. That's the kind of leader I wanted to be."

Today, 15 years later, Jose still receives messages from team members, including holiday cards with photographs of their kids. This is extremely rewarding to Jose; much more rewarding than any service plaque provided by other leaders at a close of business. Jose's experience shows his willingness and sense of obligation to be accountable for corporate decisions while also holding himself accountable to *his* vision of leadership. That's having a real, enduring impact.

In *Sustainable Leadership: Lesson of Vision, Courage, and Grit from the CEOs Who Dared to Build a Better World,* Clarke Murphy shares the story of Lynn Good, who within months of starting her new role as CEO of Duke Energy in 2014 faced an environmental disaster that resulted from one of the company's coal mines. Forty thousand tons of liquified coal ash and 27 million gallons of wastewater had leaked from a buried stormwater pipe into a local river, a source of drinking water for the communities along its bank, as well as a vital resource for local fish and wildlife.

An accountant by training, this moment had a "profound impact" on Lynn. It inspired her to move beyond her training as a "numbers gal" and to commit Duke Energy to long-term environmental sustainability. It took years, but Lynn was able to shift the company from focusing on coal to clean energy with a public goal of at least 50% carbon reduction by 2030 and net-zero carbon emissions by 2050. Today, the company is a top US renewable energy provider and is on track to operate or purchase 16,000 megawatts of renewable energy by 2025.[10] Since Lynn became CEO, Duke Energy has seen a 22% increase in revenues and a 24% increase in gross profits: Lynn is doing well, by doing good (pun intended).[11]

For both Jose and Lynn, being accountable meant more than getting the job done; it meant getting it done right for the benefit of more than just themselves or their shareholders. For these two Modern Leaders, being accountable is about being authentic to what they believe in.

Being accountable to yourself also means taking responsibility for your mistakes. Often, we misjudge the impact of our actions because we know our intent, yet others experience only our actions, explains Tasha Eurich in *Insights*. When challenged about our impact, we can drop into defensiveness, trying to explain our intent. A better choice is to draw on your humility and empathy to proactively admit and address your error.

Each of us must consider why we are here on this great earth: What is our purpose, and what are we doing to achieve it? At the end of the day, core accountability is about personal agency, purpose, and the deep truth of knowing what you can and can't live with in those last moments of your wild and precious life.

Here are four proven tactics to hold yourself accountable:

1) Articulate Your "Why"

Start by getting clear on your why, or purpose. Is there a motive greater than yourself that inspires you to do the work you do? Develop a purpose statement that can allow you to stay focused, help you prioritize more quickly, and support you to set appropriate boundaries with others. Clarity on your why will enable you to spend more time on what's meaningful to you.

Many clients and colleagues have a personal motto, or visual image they keep on their screen or in their office to reinforce their view of their best self. Peter Hawkins, professor of leadership at the University of Reading UK and international thought leader in system, team, and climate coaching, keeps a photo of his grandchildren on his desk. He says it is a reminder to leave them a planet to live on.

Our client Susan Peirick, a leader in aerospace, has a photo of a girl on her office wall to remind her of the courage she already has inside. Looking at this image, the turbulent sky above the glen and loch, the tenacious expression on the girl's face with her wind-blown hair, and her balanced stance alone on a solid stone wall help Susan feel empowered by her experience. As she continues to grow her leadership, Susan told us, "Now I have roots not in a place, but in a concept of myself—my values and vision align. I'm not at the beginning, and I'm not yet done."

2) Publicly Declare and Share Your Goals

Being public about your goals is a powerful way to build (or lose) trust. Using social media, an intranet site, or "thermometer on the wall" poster can create community support and increase visibility for your goals and goal achievement. For example, you might make public a goal to encourage colleagues to support your charitable fundraising. You may remember the ice bucket challenge that started with a dare. In 2014, Florida pro golfer Chris Kennedy recorded himself pouring a bucket of ice water over his head—and challenged several others to do the same within 24 hours. If they chickened out, they had to make a $100 donation to an ALS nonprofit. Pete Frates, a former Boston College baseball star who had been diagnosed with ALS, heard about the challenge and started promoting it on his social media channels. Soon it went viral. Hollywood actors, politicians, CEOs, and social media influencers were among those who got in on the challenge, and by the end of that summer over $115 million had been raised to fight ALS. Research shows that when you work together with others and create a group for your goals, it significantly increases your interest, resilience, and likelihood of success.[12]

3) Enlist an Accountability Partner

Don't go it alone: A study by the Association for Talent Development found that your probability of achieving a goal hinges on being specific and accountable. When you decide to pursue a goal, your chances of success fall somewhere between 10% and 25%. By sharing your goal with someone you care about, you raise the likelihood to 65%. And when you ask that person to meet with you on a regular basis to check in, your probability of success skyrockets to 95%.[13] This is why mentorship becomes so important in developing the next generation of Modern Leaders. The best mentors push their mentees to dream bigger and align their purpose with impact. Former HP and Meta Chief Marketing Officer Antonio Lucio challenged his mentee Walter Geer to think bigger when he joined advertising agency VMLY&R. "Antonio has always pushed me to see myself as more than one of the few Black men in leadership in advertising focusing on just the diversity work and initiatives. Yes, I am committed to advancing diversity in my industry, but I am also a creative first and an individual that has continued to push innovation by creating memorable, magical moments for brands. Creating incredible work and sharing it with the world is likely one of the most important vehicles of inspiration to individuals like myself that are striving for success in the advertising space."

4) Change Your Environment

If you haven't been as accountable as you would like, consider changing your process or the environment in which you are operating. It's easy to lose steam during challenging moments, especially if you're betting on willpower to get you through it all. Modern technology provides endlessly fascinating diversions for our attention, including TikTok, Instagram, video games, or our favorite distraction, binge-watching TV, which can put any person off delivering on their commitments. Research has shown that a key way to achieve your goals is to change your environment or your process for getting things done.[14] Charles Duhigg in the *Power of Habit* outlines the cue, routine, reward process. Changing your routine and changing the reward can help you increase your accountability.

For example, when the publisher's deadline loomed for the first draft of her manuscript for *Work Pause Thrive: How to Pause for Parenthood Without Killing Your Career*, Lisen knew she wouldn't be able to deliver on schedule unless she changed her environment. With her family's support, she moved across the country and lived alone for a month while her husband cared for their teenaged children and the household. Lisen was able to finish the manuscript on time and achieve her goal of becoming an author. The final reward came when readers around the world told her she gave voice to their challenges navigating work and family and provided meaningful solutions they could bring to their partners and their employers.

Accountability for Your Team and Company's Culture (Systems)

As a Modern Leader you are accountable to ensure you foster workplace cultures that enable your colleagues to thrive, but this doesn't happen in a vacuum. Your company's policies, programs, processes, and practices must also be aligned with 300% accountability. Consider the actions of Judy Marks, the CEO of Otis Worldwide, a global leader in elevator and escalator manufacturing, installation, and service. In the summer of 2020 as the world learned the horror of the murder of George Floyd, many became aware for the first time of the ongoing and persistent racial injustices faced by Black Americans. Most companies and their leaders were unprepared for the impact and trauma on their employees, especially their Black employees. Some CEOs decided to stay quiet, ignore the issue, and continue to focus on delivering business results. But others took action. Judy Marks took a public stand. On social media, she honored Otis employees like Courney Dornell who shared, for the first time publicly, his experiences of racism. Judy posted, "Your words and your stories are powerful and compelling. Let's all listen, learn, and drive change."[15]

Judy took the helm as CEO of Otis in 2017 and took the company public in April of 2020. Although Otis Elevator is focused on the commercial market and is somewhat insulated from consumer sentiments, Judy was adamant that fostering cultures of inclusion and belonging would be part of her legacy at the company. Why? Because, as Judy says, "When we look back on legacies, and you read about other leaders, at the end of the day, and I fully recognize how important creating value for our shareholders is—but this is part of it because if you can motivate and engage and have a workforce that feels so included, you will perform better. You'll perform better for your customers, you'll perform better for your shareholders, and people will genuinely want to be part of your enterprise."[16]

To be accountable to her commitment, Otis launched a new initiative, titled "Our Commitment to Change," that laid out numerous actions to ensure its 70,000 employees feel "welcome, safe and heard." The multi-pronged approach included (among other steps) an independent review of hiring, compensation and other business practices to uncover and eliminate biases; anti-racism, unconscious bias, and inclusion learning at all levels of the company; a commitment to diversity metrics across the company, and the creation of a new advisory group, Perspectives on Inclusion. All of these initiatives were designed to build accountability and trust across Otis.

Where is the company today? Judy has made significant strides in diversifying her leadership team: 44% of senior executives are women and 50% are people of color. According to its 2022 ESG report, Otis is on track to achieve gender parity in executive ranks by 2030, six of its 10 board members identify as women, racially diverse, or both, and employee ratings of inclusive culture reached 72%. Otis received the following designations:

- The World's Top Female-Friendly Companies—Forbes, 2022;
- World's Best Employers—Forbes, 2022;
- America's Most Responsible Companies—Newsweek, 2022 and 2023;
- Best Places to Work for LGBTQ+ Equality—Human Rights Campaign Foundation, 2022.

Judy Marks's commitment to a culture of inclusivity and belonging is one example of holding yourself and your team accountable. As another example, consider how our client, the CEO of a regional transportation hub, handled a tough situation.

The CEO made a public commitment to create economic growth for the region through a construction project that would create jobs for local workers in the near term and retail opportunities from increased traffic in the long term. As this multi-year modernization project was underway, she ran into a challenge in holding her team accountable and called us in to support the group with team coaching. The executive team was committed to 300% accountability—being people-first leaders, achieving their business goals, and contributing to society—and yet one of their peers was violating the team norms.

One of the leaders, we'll call her Rhonda, was on-target to achieve her goals, but to obtain results, she was burning bridges with her peers and leaving a wake of destruction lower in the organization. Rhonda was a classic example of a "toxic rock star"—an employee who delivers great results but whose attitude and behavior creates a toxic culture for those who work with or for them.

We shared research by Christine Porath, author of *Mastering Civility*, which showed that when leaders are uncivil (not treating their employees with respect), their teams are less motivated and less productive. One study revealed that a toxic rock star results in 66% of employees cutting back their efforts, 80% losing time worrying about their workplace experience, with 12% leaving their jobs. In contrast, those leaders who were civil had teams which delivered 13% higher performance.[17] These negative impacts were a wake-up call for our client and her executive team.

To learn more about their strengths and vulnerabilities as Modern Leaders, the team participated in a HEARTI 360° Team assessment, which uncovered a challenge in accountability across the team and especially for Rhonda. A peer noted: "Rhonda is decisive and takes accountability. It often seems like she is taking accountability almost too far, where she is trying to do it all on her own. She works with other departments, but it can feel like she is directing them rather than collaborating. It feels demeaning."

Another shared, "Rhonda is confident in her decision-making and would rather make a decision and go by herself, rather than seek out different perspectives. It's demotivating, no one person has the best answer all of the time."

Although Rhonda was a high performer, the CEO was deeply concerned about the impact on the team and culture. She was eager to help her executive team operate as Modern Leaders, but Rhonda was stuck in a Traditional Leader mindset and behaviors. The CEO had a candid conversation about Rhonda's achievements in delivering measured results and the cost to the team of how she achieved those results. The CEO set clear expectations on performance to values and mapped out how Rhonda could succeed, but Rhonda was not interested or able to evolve her behavior. She found a new job at a company whose culture was more aligned with her Traditional Leadership approach.

Modern Leaders hold team members and peers accountable to their shared values and impact on culture.

Our client's actions are a good example of 300% accountability when it comes to company systems. If you want to create a company driven by triple bottom-line impact, you must link values, mission, and purpose to the company culture. Retaining high performing toxic rock stars who operate with a Traditional Leader mindset will hinder your success.

The Importance of Feedback

Some leaders find it difficult to hold others accountable by providing developmental feedback. According to Lean In and McKinsey & Company, women are more than 20% less likely than men to say their manager gave them critical feedback that contributed to their growth.[18] And according to another recent survey, Black and Latinx employees are more likely to receive feedback about their personality than the actual quality of their job performance.[19] This lack of feedback can be linked to a common workplace phenomenon that Morehouse President and former Harvard University Professor Dr. David A. Thomas refers to as *protective hesitation*.[20]

Protective hesitation is when a leader fails to give constructive criticism to an employee out of fear of being perceived as racist, sexist, homophobic, or any other prejudice. While the intent behind this action may seem like a good idea for leaders hoping to avoid having difficult conversations, the reality is that this feedback style does more harm than good to an individual's success.

Being a leader means having the courage to have those difficult conversations. As we shared in Chapter 4, "Be Empathetic," Dr. Brené Brown argues that, "Clear is kind. Unclear is unkind."[21] If you truly want to help develop diverse talent, you need to build your skill at delivering feedback kindly and clearly.

Leader Tool Kit

How to Embed 300% Accountability into Your Team's Goals

To drive true team impact, embedding 300% accountability into your team's goals is essential. Here are four steps to uplevel your team's impact:

1) Support Your Team With Three Key Mindset Shifts

300% accountability requires team members to understand their work and efforts is about delivering results that will impact more than themselves. Help your team understand the following:

- "Instead of only being accountable for *my* deliverables, I am responsible for supporting others to achieve our collective goals."
- "Their success is my success"
- "My success is our success"

(continued)

2) Gain Team Alignment On What Successful Impact Looks Like

Ask your team:

- What is the business result we need to achieve?
- Beyond our specific business objectives, who or what can benefit from our efforts?
- How can we achieve triple bottom line impact?
- Who can we partner/collaborate with to achieve our goals?
- What measurable outcomes will enable us to track our progress?
- What roadblocks might keep us from achieving our goals?
- What does success look like?

3) Gain Clarity On How You Can Support Your Team

Ask yourself:

- Who would benefit most from leading this project?
- How can I support them to deliver 300% accountability?
- What do they need to know to achieve successful impact?
- Have I given them sufficient authority?
- Have I informed the key stakeholders of our plans and who is in charge?
- How am I helping the team stay on track?
- How am I helping the team communicate our progress?

4) Celebrate Success

Finally, plan for success:

- How will we celebrate success?
- How will we communicate our successful impact?
- How will we recognize each other?

Accountability to the Broader World (Society)

Remember *Fearless Girl*? That statue of a little girl hands on her hips defiantly facing down the Wall Street Bull in New York City. It showed up one day out of nowhere and captured the world's attention. It became a powerful symbol of female leadership in business. It also became an embodiment of "girl power," and within weeks of its debut thousands of little girls flocked to have their picture taken beside the statue.

The statue was part of a marketing campaign launched by State Street Global Advisors as part of its aggressive push to increase the number of women in prominent leadership positions. State Street called on companies to increase the number of women on their boards and to invest in companies that had women CEOs. The campaign garnered headlines, won awards, and appeared to be a resounding success. That is until it was discovered that the bank only had three women on its 11-member board of directors and only five women on its 28-member leadership team. Oh, and State Street was in the middle of not one but three (!) pay equity lawsuits when the *Fearless Girl* debuted.

Talk about a public relations nightmare. *Fearless Girl* has since become a ringing example of performative marketing. Exactly the kind of company action that breeds mistrust and one of the key reasons 59% of consumers will not buy a product or brand if they don't trust the company that sells it.[22] It's not just companies that are being challenged. Consumers around the globe also don't trust CEOs. According to the Edelman Trust Barometer (an annual analysis of consumer trust in institutions and brands the public relations agency has been running since 2001), only 47% of US consumers believe CEOs are telling the truth. CEO credibility has hit rock bottom in countries such as Japan and France where only 18% and 22%, respectively, trust business leaders. In fact, Edelman found that 56% of global consumers agree that "business leaders are purposely trying to mislead people by saying things they know are false or gross exaggerations."[23]

This is where 300% accountability comes in. Remember in Chapter 1, "Everything's Changed," when we talked about the role of the corporation shifting from shareholder to stakeholder value? This isn't just about PR, it's about being a modern workplace that requires Modern Leaders who can be humble, empathetic *and* accountable. It requires balance between business outcomes, desired behaviors, and social impact outcomes.

How do you do that? Align your company's purpose and values to drive greater impact than just delivering profits to shareholders, set goals that help reinforce that purpose and those values, make it public so you are held to your words through deeds, and then *act* accordingly.

Take Salesforce as an example of how a company can put people, the planet, and prosperity for all as core tenets of its operations. In 2019, the company leaders set and published a series of goals to drive business and social change. Their equality goals focused on increasing representation of Black, Latine, Indigenous, and multiracial employees in the US and of women employees globally. The company has been pursuing a series of representation goals, initially announced in 2019, including having 50% of US employees from underrepresented groups, doubling the representation of Black leaders, increasing representation of minority leaders by 50%, and increasing US representation of underrepresented minorities by 50% by 2023. Salesforce also announced in August 2022 that it has already surpassed the first of these goals.[24]

Salesforce's sustainability measures include supporting a healthy planet by reducing air travel emissions and increasing spend with suppliers who have signed Salesforce's Sustainability Exhibit. The exhibit includes several obligations for suppliers, most notably requiring them to commit to setting a science-based target to reduce greenhouse gas (GHG) emissions aligned with the Science Based Targets initiative (SBTi). Salesforce set a goal to maintain employee business travel emissions intensity below 50% of its FY20 baseline. The 2022 Salesforce Stakeholder Impact Report showed that goal was achieved, and absolute emissions continue to decline.[25]

> *Salesforce believes that business is the greatest platform for change. Our commitment to equality and sustainability helps us be a better company—and foster more inclusive, equitable, and resilient communities.*
>
> **—Suzanne DiBianca, EVP,**
> **chief impact officer, Salesforce**

When it comes to prosperity for all, Salesforce starts within. The company has long had an implicit commitment to pay equity, but it all came to a head in 2015 when Cindy Robbins, Saleforce's employee success chief, and Lela Seka, another Salesforce senior leader, challenged CEO Marc Benioff by arguing, "We need to determine if pay inequality exists here." As Marc writes in his book *TrailBlazer: The Power of Business as the Greatest Platform for Change,* "I'm sure the look on my face betrayed the mix of indignation and astonishment I was feeling. I'll admit my defensiveness was welling up."

Marc had been on a long campaign to increase the number of women in leadership at his company. In 2012 he launched an initiative called Women Surge to ensure the company could boast at least 30% women at every level of the organization. Why 30%? Because he knew companies that rank in the top quartile for diversity in leadership were 33% more likely to be profitable than those that ranked lower.[26] He was proud of the progress his company was making but knew it had a long way to go. (Note: in 2022, Salesforce committed to ensuring that 40% of its global employees identify as women.)

With that challenge, Salesforce conducted internal research and discovered that, yes, pay inequity was an issue. It promptly made adjustments and has every year since. In 2022, Salesforces announced, "Our analysis found 8.5% of our global employees required adjustments. Of those, 92% were based on gender globally, and 8% were based on race or ethnicity in the US. As a result, we spent $5.6 million to address any unexplained differences in pay, a total of more than $22 million spent since 2015."[27]

Businesses with cultures strong in 300% accountability deliver better business results.

Profits? Don't worry, investors are doing just fine. In March 2022, "We had another phenomenal quarter and full-year of financial results," Marc Benioff announced. "As we continue to see tremendous demand from customers, we're raising our FY23 revenue guidance to $32.1 billion at the high-end of range, with non-GAAP operating margin of 20%, and operating cash flow growth of 22% year-over-year."[28]

Bringing it back to the leadership, because Salesforce understands that change does not happen in a vacuum, the company ties a portion of executive variable pay to ESG performance. Salesforce is *the* model of 300% accountability—leaders accountable to themselves, the company, and their communities.

You Need to Know

300% Accountability Is a Must for Every Stage of Business

Having clear priorities and goals to support a diverse workforce, responsible products, and a sustainable planet are essential in every stage of business, they're not just for mega-corporations.

- In start-ups where everyone needs to be pulling in the same direction, these goals are a survival tool, keeping everyone focused on the top priority. In addition, sustainability and diversity goals give investors a yardstick for measuring success of their investment, enhancing the opportunity for future investment rounds.

- In medium-sized, rapidly scaling organizations, the goals provide a common language for execution. They clarify expectations and keep employees aligned horizontally and vertically.

- In larger companies, the goals can help demolish silos and cultivate connections among far-flung contributors. Publicly stated, they can encourage teams to keep stretching for more, driving increased innovation.

As we've explained, accountability today is far more nuanced than it was for previous generations of leaders. To be truly committed to delivering triple bottom-line impact, Modern Leaders must expand their definition of accountability. For a Modern Leader, 300% accountability doesn't stop with yourself or your team. It expands outward to ensure your company drives impact by living its values and purpose each and every day. This requires embedding your company's mission and values into your company's programs, policies, and practices.

Then you must hold yourself and your colleagues accountable to the shared value of sustainable impact. For being a true Modern Leader, 300% accountability is a foundational power skill.

Reframe

300% Accountability Is a Power Skill

- Keeps you focused on your purpose;
- Reinforces your humility as a you look beyond *your specific goals* to deliverables that make impact;
- Builds trust;
- Promotes getting the right things done, the right way;
- Fosters workplace cultures of inclusion;
- Ensures company programs, policies, and practices are aligned with company mission and purpose;
- Delivers on triple bottom-line goals.

Evolving Your Leadership

Ten Ways to Increase Your Accountability

Yourself:

1) Get clear on your why, and articulate your purpose to your team;

2) Publicly declare and share your goals. Walk your own talk—make and meet your commitments;

3) Don't go it alone, find an accountability partner;

4) Change your environment to help sustain your efforts.

Your Team:

5) Utilize leader's intent: be clear on the goal, flexible on the path;

6) Give timely feedback and recognition for both the what (results) and the how (behavior);

7) Promote a culture of mutual support.

Your Community/the World:

8) Publish company-wide targets and regular progress updates to all stakeholders;

9) Create internal systems aligned for positive global impact;

10) Leverage external tools to measure progress (Syndio, Culture Amp, Dandi, NIST Greenhouse Gas, Sustainability Accounting Standards Board [SASB], etc.).

6

Be Resilient: Because the World Needs You

U.S. Surgeon General, Dr. Vivek Murthy, is no newcomer to the challenges of leadership, but he made headlines when he revealed in a 2023 New York Times op-ed that he had suffered mental health challenges as a result of loneliness. He wrote, "Loneliness—like depression, with which it can be associated—can chip away at your self-esteem and erode your sense of who you are. That's what happened to me."[1]

Ten years ago, heck, even five years ago, you wouldn't have heard people talking openly in a work environment about the feelings of isolation, stress, and the challenges of mental health. Rarely have we heard leaders talking vulnerably about the deep pain of living many of us struggle with each and every day. Yes, it is about mental health, but it's also about work and its role in our lives. The fact that leaders such as Vivek are now sharing their experiences, and doing so without shame and worry that others won't think they are strong and capable, may be the only silver lining from the devastation of the global pandemic and the myriad of other crises that have impacted the workplace in the past number of years.

In his book *The End of Burnout; Why Work Drains Us and How to Build Better Lives,* Jonathan Malesic argues that we have all bought into a "noble lie" about work, productivity, and self-worth.[2] This "noble lie," according to Jonathan, is the belief that "work is the path to self-actualization. The ideal that motivates us to work to the point of burnout is the promise that if you work hard, you will live a good life: not just a life of material comfort, but a life of social dignity, moral character and spiritual purpose."[3]

"We who live in the system can rarely see it," writes Jonathan. "We take its norms for granted, like the air we breathe."

What exactly are those norms? Joan C. Williams, Sullivan Professor of Law and founding director of the Center for Work-Life Law at the University of California Law, San Francisco, says one of the key issues we face is the pressure to be the "ideal worker"—that person who is work devoted and who has the capacity to arrive early, stay late, pull all-nighters, work weekends, and remain tied to their electronic devices 24/7. How can they do this? In part because any family obligations are taken care of by someone at home.

In the past, the ideal worker has typically been a man—usually a white man—who is married to a woman and who is the primary breadwinner for the family. According to Joan, "The concept reflects a breadwinner-homemaker model that dates back to the Industrial Revolution and functioned fairly well through the 1960s, until women began entering the formal workforce in greater numbers."[4] Joan argues that our modern workplaces are still structured around the "ideal worker" model and are the key to why so many of us feel overwhelmed and struggle.

Business professors Lakshimi Ramarajan and Erin Reed argue, "To be ideal workers, people must choose, again and again, to prioritize their jobs ahead of other parts of their lives: their role as parents (actual or anticipated), their personal needs, and even their health. This reality is difficult to talk about, let alone challenge, because despite the well-documented personal and physical costs of these choices, an overwhelming number of people believe that achieving success *requires* them, and those around them, to conform to this ideal."[5] For the vast majority of us who are unable—or unwilling—to operate like ideal workers, the consequences to our careers and our self-esteem, as Jonathan Malesic makes clear, can be dire.

Enter, resiliency.

Grit Versus Resiliency

Before we dive deep into the definition of resiliency, it's important to separate it from its darker twin: grit.

You may be one of the 29 million—and counting—viewers of psychology professor Angela Duckworth's 2013 TED Talk on grit. She maps out the research she conducted on the importance of hard work, perseverance, and success. She looked at teachers, children, sales and business executives and, as she tells the audience, "In all of those very different contexts, one characteristic emerged that was a significant predictor of success. It wasn't social intelligence, it wasn't good looks, physical health, and it wasn't I.Q. It was grit."[6]

As Angela explains, "Grit is living life like it is a marathon, not a sprint." Grit, she says, is having sustained stamina. She went on to write the best-selling book *Grit: The Power of Passion and Perseverance*, which has come to be essential reading in many business schools and workplaces. Grit, as one of our PrismWork colleagues—a repeat chief people officer—says, has become "religion for business leaders."

The dictionary defines grit as "unyielding courage in the face of hardship; resolve; strength of character." Sounds great, right? Who doesn't want to have strong character, courage, and the resolve to overcome hardship. But there is a dark side to the religion of grit—and that is the impact it has on our well-being and its focus on personal achievement rather than collective impact.

The problem with grit as it has been interpreted is that it lacks a moral compass and lacks a social construct. It is completely focused on personal success—and by "success" we mean achievement. In a workplace setting, grit then becomes about competition versus collaboration. It becomes about being the ideal worker so you—and you alone—can rise to the top. Grit in this context does not make room for imposter syndrome or the complexity of work and family obligations or the trauma of burnout. In fact, by definition, those who burn out lack the implied moral courage and fortitude necessary for grit.

Another challenge with grit as it is defined is that it doesn't take into account the social, economic, and political realities that each of us must navigate. Do white children born into poverty who can't manage to graduate from high school because their parents are addicted to oxycontin lack grit? Do black children whose brothers are murdered by police officers and can't manage to pull themselves up by the proverbial bootstraps lack grit? Is the reason that white men still make up 89% of Fortune 500 CEOs and that 70% of board positions in publicly traded companies are held by men because women lack grit?

We don't think so. Do you?

Grit can become the false god that forces you, and your team, to never give up. You've heard the term "'Til you drop"—shop, dance, party, work. It doesn't matter what it is, the meta-narrative is as a hustler, you go hard and nonstop with any task no matter how much rejection, fatigue, or how many obstacles you face. Grit can force you into persistence when the resilient answer is to forge another path.

Do the best you can until you know better. Then when you know better, do better.

—Maya Angelou, poet and author

At PrismWork, we believe in perseverance and passion and sustained commitment, but we also understand that each of us operates within a construct. Rather than just powering through with grit, we focus on building resilience, supporting leaders in their ability to bend and bounce forward after they have struggled, faltered, or failed. We help them understand that persistence—grit—is a way of coping with current difficulties, which is useful for near-term results. But in an ever-changing environment, a Modern Leader's focus must be on strengthening future performance and impact by building resiliency.

Consider Ping Fu, Inc. Magazine's 2005 Entrepreneur of the Year.[7] Born on the eve of China's Cultural Revolution, she was separated from her family at the age of eight and grew up in a government dormitory along with other children whose parents were accused of "pro-capitalist" tendencies. Eventually, she found her way to the United States. She landed in New Mexico with no money and only a few spoken English words: thank you, hello, and help. A love of problem-solving led her to computer science, and Fu became part of the team that created NCSA Mosaic, which became Netscape. She then started a company, Geomagic, which she sold to 3D Systems in 2013. Today, she spends her time advising other entrepreneurs and advocating for more women in STEM careers. She serves on the NACIE (National Advisory Council on Innovation and Entrepreneurship) at the Department of Commerce, and she is an active supporter of the White House's Office of Science and Technology Policy. She has won numerous awards including Outstanding American by Choice award from the US Citizenship and Immigration Services (USCIS).[8]

In her book *Bend, Not Break: A Life in Two Worlds*, Ping Fu writes that she believes resilience is like bamboo: those who cultivate resilience are agile, adaptable, and have the "ability to bounce back even from the most difficult times." She goes on to write that she has learned the greatest reward as a leader to be in service. Leadership, according to Ping Fu, is about "focusing on a better outcome for your team and promoting your teammates." She links resilience and leadership by focusing on how resiliency enables you to deliver your life's purpose in the service of others.[9]

In the winter of 2023, three high-profile leaders quit their high-profile roles: New Zealand Prime Minister Jacinda Ardern, Scottish Prime Minister Nicola Sturgeon, and YouTube CEO Susan Wojicicki. When Jacinda made her resignation announcement, she said, "I am human, politicians are human. We give all that we can for as long as we can. And then it's time. And for me, it's time."[10] Nicola said she knows the "time is now" for her to stand down, adding that it is "right for me, for my party and for the country."[11] Susan wrote in an open letter to employees, "After nearly 25 years here, I've decided to step back from my role as the head of YouTube and start a new chapter focused on my family, health, and personal projects I'm passionate about."[12]

> **Modern Leaders build resiliency not just for their own careers and success but so they can use their experiences and abilities to make a difference for others.**

What do they have in common? Yes, they all identify as women, but more importantly, they all are modeling Modern Leadership built on HEARTI principles. These leaders don't lack grit, they have powered through years of challenges and the pressures of being at the top of their chosen professions. It takes humility to say, "I can no longer be on this path," and it takes courage to say, "I'm going to pivot and do something else."

A few last things about grit, burnout, and resilience:

- **Grit can become a distraction**

  If you are tenaciously focused on overcoming one obstacle—or even a few obstacles—you may lose sight of the big picture. The result? You become less agile, less able to know when enough is enough and look for another solution or approach. Remember, it's not about the trees, it's about the forest. Grow yours with bamboo.

- **Burnout keeps you from making an impact**

  If you're constantly burning through your reserves, you are much less likely to be able to make a meaningful impact that benefits all stakeholders. As they say on airplanes, put on your oxygen mask first. By doing so, you'll be better able to help and serve others.

- **Resilience can be a key source of growth**

  Research has shown that after facing deep challenges, many people experience significant post-traumatic growth. Dr. Steven M. Southwick, professor emeritus of psychiatry, PTSD, and resilience at Yale University School of Medicine and coauthor of the book *Resilience: The Science of Mastering Life's Greatest Challenges*, explains that if you can cope today with all that's happening in the world around you, then when you are on the other side of it, you'll be stronger.[13]

- **Resilience is a team sport**

  A quick way to ensure you'll burn out is to try and do everything yourself. By micromanaging everything, not only do you burn out, you also take away the opportunity for others to learn and grow by partnering with you to solve the problem. You can build your resilience and your team's resilience by collaborating together to achieve your mutually agreed upon goals—and, don't forget to ask for help!

Resiliency—It's Nuanced

In Chapter 2, "Intentional Power," we introduced you to Deepa Purushothaman who was one of the youngest people and first Indian American woman to be named partner at the prestigious consulting firm Deloitte. She spent over 20 years rising up the ladder, taking on bigger and more challenging responsibilities, and bearing the hidden weight of representing women, and specifically, women of color. Through the years, she suffered health issues, but she carried on because she didn't want to let her heritage or her gender down as one of the first, the few, the only at her level. Finally, not long after she celebrated her 20th anniversary at the company, she began to question her choices and her responsibilities.

"I asked myself for whom, and to whom, was I obligated to continue to suffer and realized being resilient meant having the courage to leave and uncover what other ways I might be able to be of service to my community," Deepa told our students during her visit to our Stanford Continuing Studies class.

As we previously shared, after she left Deloitte, Deepa went on to write a best-selling book and cofounded nFormation, a company dedicated to supporting women of color who are leaders in their organizations. Deepa explained to the class, "The concept of resiliency means different things to different groups. Racism in our culture forces Black and Brown people to be more resilient—a pressure they don't want or need. Add to that other intersectional challenges—being a woman, being an immigrant, being part of the LGTBQ+ community—and you can imagine why being resilient is its own burden."

For example, in the research we did with Deepa and nFormation, we saw that Black women who self-identify as highly resilient (88% in our survey) still struggle with the pressure of resiliency in the workplace. As one Black C-suite leader told us, "My executive team is made up of all white men. I am the only woman on the team and for many of them, I am the only Black person they have ever met or worked with. I'm constantly navigating the challenge of both fitting into the majority culture while representing 'all' Black people and 'all' women. It's exhausting and it's affecting my health."

We heard similar stories from immigrant Latinas and first-generation Chinese American women. They told us they felt their careers had been hampered by stereotypes about their people and cultures. One Asian American woman told us, "Today's systems were designed by yesterday's men: White men with stay-at-home wives. But what about the rest of us? There's no place for me here." Another woman, a Latina who had immigrated from El Salvador, said, "Every time we show up, there's that little questioning of who we are. Our capabilities. Sometimes it can be really challenging."

Sociologists, psychologists, and other experts have begun to consider resilience in the context of race, ethnicity, and other determining factors. In their abstract, "Revisiting 'resilience' in light of racism, 'othering' and resistance," Wendy Sims-Schouten and Patricia Gilbert argue "that current definitions of resilience need to be redefined and reconceptualized particularly in settings dominated by white middle-class voices that define what 'positive emotions,' 'successful traits' and 'coping mechanisms' entail."[14] Ijeoma Madabutu studies culturally informed risk and protective factors for mood disturbance and suicide behavior in African American communities. She says, "While resilience is an important protective factor to highlight, it is crucial to validate how harmful chronic exposure to race-based stressors is for African Americans even when they exhibit resilience."[15]

As a Modern Leader, you must consider the systems in which you and your team operate and how that affects hiring, retention, and day-to-day well-being and productivity. For example, consider your own C-suite and leadership team. Is it diverse? For instance, are there equal numbers of women and men?

As a Modern Leader, it's imperative you understand that resiliency is nuanced so you can fully support your teams to do their best work—and thrive.

If not, why not? If there are no women, is that because women are less resilient? We think not. As one PowHER Redefined research respondent said to us, "If markets were efficient—meaning if meritocracy was real—we'd see more women in leadership." Clearly something is up.

The Core Traits of Resilient Leaders

Academic research around the concept of resilience started about 40 years ago with pioneering studies by Professor Norman Garmezy. He studied Holocaust victims, survivors of natural disasters, and children of schizophrenic parents who did *not* suffer psychological illness as a result of their parents' mental illness. He concluded resilience played a greater role in mental health than anyone had previously suspected. His focus on resilience has been expanded and applied to teams, organizations, even countries.

The collective research on resilient leaders has revealed six core traits that enable them to thrive. Resilient leaders:

- **Are Intrinsically Motivated**

    From his studies of survivors, Professor Norman Garmezy also concluded that people with an "internal locus of control," that is, those who believe that their own agency drives their life experiences instead of being at the whim of external circumstances, are more likely to be resilient in adverse situations.[16] These leaders' motivation to engage in behaviors are driven by inherent satisfaction of the activity, rather than a reward or specific outcome.

- **Are Self-Aware**

    Daniel Goleman[17], psychologist and author of the best-selling book *Emotional Intelligence*, has said that resilient leaders require a healthy dose of self-awareness, as well as an awareness of those around them to manage relationships and sustain change in the face of uncertainty. By being self-aware, resilient leaders know what is important to them, why they are doing what they are doing, and when they need to stop. This enables them to prevent burnout and to stay mission-focused.

- **Have a Pragmatic Acceptance of Reality**

    We might call them pessimistic optimists or optimistic pessimists because resilient leaders focus on discovering the reality of a situation for themselves and their team. They do so to understand the obstacles and to determine which are worth their time and which are intractable. Journalist Diane Coutu has written extensively on resilience. In a piece for *Harvard Business Review* she explains, "When we truly stare down reality, we prepare ourselves to act in ways that allow us to endure extreme hardship."[18] On a lighter note, when we shared this in class, one of our students reminded us of the old joke, "How do you eat an elephant? One bite at a time."

■ Are Able to Improvise

Resilient leaders are masters of improvisation and creative problem-solving. They understand there are a myriad of ways to tackle a problem, and as a result, they encourage their teams to operate with "leaders intent" by focusing on the end result or outcome needed rather than insisting their employees rigidly follow a preset path. This promotes innovation, collaboration, and agile thinking. "Leader's intent" is essential in shape-shifting, non-hierarchical, flexible organizations where workers are empowered to devise the most effective path to the goal.

■ Are Altruistic

Research has shown that resilient people have a concern for others and a degree of selflessness. They have a pay-it-forward approach and don't expect reward for their actions. They are often dedicated to causes they find meaningful and that give them a sense of purpose.[19] Resilient leaders don't survive for their own benefit, they thrive so they can help others.

■ Have a Deep Belief That Life Is Meaningful

Resilient leaders devise constructs about suffering they experience in the moment as part of some sort of greater meaning. They build bridges from today's problems to a fuller, more constructed life. It's called meaning-making. Those bridges make the present manageable—removing the sense that the present is overwhelming. They provide context for the immediate challenge, as a potential gift to a greater future. Viktor E. Frankl, an Austrian psychiatrist and Auschwitz survivor, provides context for meaning-making in his book *Man's Search for Meaning*. To survive, Frankl realized he had to find some purpose. He did so by imagining himself giving a lecture after the war on the psychology of the concentration camp, to help outsiders understand what he and so many others had been through. Although he wasn't even sure he would survive, Frankl created concrete goals for himself. In doing so, he succeeded in rising above the sufferings of the moment.

Increasing Your Resiliency

Research has shown that resilient leaders are more likely to experience positive emotions and less likely to experience negative emotions. They are more open to new experiences. They tend to be more outgoing, socially connected, and integrated with their communities.[20] Sounds great, doesn't it? Who wouldn't want to be resilient? But there is a lot of confusion about our tendency toward resiliency. Is it nature or nurture?

Resilience appears to be dictated by a combination of genetics, personal history, environment, and situational context. So far, research has found the genetic part to be relatively small. Karestan Koenen, professor of psychiatric epidemiology at Harvard's T.H. Chan School of Public Health, has explained, "The way I think about it is that there are temperamental or personality characteristics that are genetically influenced, like risk-taking, or whether you're an introvert or extrovert."[21]

So while there appears to be a genetic component to resiliency, it is not exclusively genetic.[22] What's most important to know is that it can be learned.

Here are eight ways you can increase your resiliency:

1) Fail

Seriously. We aren't joking. The first step to growing resilience is to fail. Once you've failed, you have the opportunity to find the gift in the experience, including gaining confidence in your ability to handle the next failure.[23] Failures don't have to be huge and life altering. For example, getting a tough question in the middle of your presentation to the CEO and not having the best answer is a micro-failure. These micro-failures provide the opportunity to demonstrate micro-resilience—recentering and moving forward. Of course, there are more significant failures that require deeper self-reflection and time to recover. Robbing yourself of the chance of failure means you aren't pushing yourself and you aren't giving yourself the chance to learn how to be resilient. So go out there . . . and fail.

> *I have not failed 10,000 times—I've successfully found 10,000 ways that will not work.*
>
> **—Thomas Edison on inventing the light bulb**

Leader Tool Kit

How to Navigate Failure to Increase Resilience

Positive psychologist Martin Seligman has found that there are 3 Ps that can help us to see the light at the end of a dark tunnel of setbacks: personalization, pervasiveness, and permanence.[24] To move through failure and claim your gift of resilience, ask yourself these three core questions to get perspective:

- What factors (mine, others, external forces) contributed to this failure? (Personalization) While humble leaders take ownership for their stumbles, studies show that

(continued)

considering all elements of a situation can make you stronger by reducing blame and self-criticism. You may also discover ways to change the system to avoid future failures. Getting a more accurate view of what happened allows you to recover—and even to thrive.

- Will this setback spread to all aspects of my life or is it affecting one area? (Pervasiveness) Your whole life probably isn't falling apart simultaneously. Naming the affected area right-sizes the impact and might prompt an idea for an action you can take to recover. In addition, identifying bright spots in other areas of your life and expressing gratitude for them will give you hope. Looking at the whole context helps you have perspective on the setback.

- Will this last forever? (Permanence) Someone's passing is permanent, but your feelings at this moment don't have to be. The belief that you'll forever suffer as a result of an event causes yourself more harm than the actual event. Accept your current feelings as normal, and expect they will change over time.

2) Build in Moments of Micro-Resilience

A small way to increase daily resiliency is to build in mini-breaks and establish boundaries. Our clients often find doing breathing exercises—mini-meditations—before clicking "join" for the next meeting is a way to build micro-resiliency. In days where working from home means there is no break between the "office" and home life, JeanAnn has invented "the commute." Before she starts work each morning, she takes a short walk around the block. At the end of each workday, she reverses that walk around the block. This boundary making enables JeanAnn to shift her mindset from home to work and back again. Figure out some ways you can create micro-resilience to help you through the day, and don't forget to acknowledge yourself for your efforts.

3) Anticipate Outcomes

In his 2015 TED Talk "How to Stay Calm When You Know You'll Be Stressed," neuroscientist David Levitan, explained that anticipating outcomes by doing a "pre-mortem" is a powerful way to increase your resilience. When under stress, our amygdala gets hijacked, and we aren't able to make thoughtful, calm decisions. We became reactive, not proactive. Neuroscience research shows us that when we predict obstacles and brainstorm potential solutions, we don't drop into "fight, flight, or freeze" mode, which means we are able to drive better outcomes.[25]

One of the most impactful exercises for a team to build resiliency is to perform a pre-mortem, anticipating what might go wrong with a project and building indicators to prompt course corrections that will increase the likelihood of success. First, imagine your project failed. Ask the team to brainstorm what went wrong. Bring "AWE," a sense of wonder and curiosity to the discussion, by asking, "And what else . . .?" Ask the question several times, to uncover the problem behind the problem. List out all the things that could go wrong. Then consider how you might have known the project was headed for failure. With your long list of things that could go wrong, brainstorm metrics for each that you can track that indicate the project is headed for a failure. On the problems you deem most likely, prepare a corrective action plan. Pre-mortems don't only have to be about navigating the negative. You can also imagine the most positive outcome and prepare for extraordinary success. What if your project is wildly successful and you have an overflow of customers? What if tomorrow your CFO offered you $100,000 to invest in a project? Do you have a plan to capitalize on the opportunity? The point here is to practice emotional regulation and build a sense of equilibrium for the range of situations life brings you.

Leader Tool Kit

How to Conduct a Pre-mortem

- Imagine an upcoming project and its conclusion.
- The project failed.
- What went wrong?
- Bring "AWE" (Ask: And what else?)
- How could we have known?

Note: Pre-mortems don't only have to be about navigating the negative. You can also imagine the most positive outcome and prepare for that as well. The point here is emotional regulation and building a sense of equilibrium for all that life brings you.

4) Stay in the "Now" and Focus on Things You Can Control

In her moving memoir *Smacked: A Story of White-Collar Ambition, Addiction, and Tragedy*, Eilene Zimmerman writes about how an unimaginable tragedy—the death of her ex-husband from an overdose—shaped her life and her children's lives. She says, "When I was still in the thick of it, five years ago, I felt overwhelmed and hopeless, weighed down by worries. The way I got through that was to narrow my thinking. Instead of worrying about what life would be like next week or month or year—I worked hard to stay focused on the here and now and not give in to ruminations about the past or the future, which I couldn't change or control."[26] Focusing on what you can control will help you get through the immediate challenge so that, like Eilene, one day you might be able to look back and realize that the trauma you experienced did pass and may have even led to post-traumatic growth.

5) Get Comfortable with Change

One phrase attributed to the Greek philosopher Heraclitus is "The only thing constant is change." Over the last several years, we have seen a dramatic amount of change in the workplace, as the global pandemic drove many to work from home, to a call to return to the office, to shifts in advice from medical experts and pushback from employees, which led to delayed return to the office. Schools were in session remotely, back on campus, and then remote again for a period of time. What was the one constant thing through all of this? Change. The reason so many of us are afraid of change is because it means we are out of control. Resilience is only necessary because life is filled with things we can't control, change is inevitable, so getting comfortable with change is fundamental to being resilient.

> *I believe life is like a journey on a mountain range. It goes up and down, and at each peak the view is different. So if you feel stuck and want to go to a different peak you have to go down before you can go up.*
>
> —Ping Fu,[27] entrepreneur and author of
> ***Bend, Not Break: A Life in Two Worlds***

6) Make Peace with Anxiety

Guy Raz, award-winning journalist and host of the *How I Built This* podcast, which has more than 19 million downloads each month, has spent the majority of his career in the spotlight. Either online, on camera, or onstage, Guy has interviewed hundreds of innovators and entrepreneurs including Patagonia founder Yvon Chouinard, Spanx billionaire Sarah Blakely, and Airbnb cofounder Joe Gebbia. And yet, Guy says, "I get nervous every time. I now understand anxiety is part of the process." Morra Aarons-Mele, author of *The Anxious Achiever: Turn Your Biggest Fears into Your Leadership Superpower*, says, "Part of building resilience is knowing that anxiety is a natural part of living for many of us so rather than fight it, make peace with it. Being a resilient leader is about getting up and doing it again and again even when you are feeling anxious or are filled with self-doubt."[28]

7) Be Grateful

It is nearly impossible to be grateful in the midst of trauma, but a meta-analysis of research published in the *International Journal of Social Psychiatry* found a correlation between gratitude, resilience, and feelings of happiness. By practicing daily gratitude, you are less likely to be overwhelmed when a crisis does happen. It has been shown that gratitude builds emotional resilience by:

- Helping us to see the positive things in life;
- Fighting the negative ruminations and replacing pessimistic thoughts with optimistic ones;
- Staying grounded and accepting the present situation, even if that is a harsh reality;
- Identifying and focusing only on solutions;
- Maintaining good health by regulating our metabolic functioning and by controlling the hormonal imbalances;
- Sustaining relationships and appreciating people who are there for us. As a result, we feel more loved, cared for, and more hopeful.[29]

8) Be Kind to Yourself

Clinical psychologist Dr. Raphael Rose, who serves as the associate director of the UCLA Anxiety and Depression Research Center, says self-compassion is essential to resilience. Failing, picking yourself up, learning from your mistakes, and having patience at how many times you mess up as you try to change are all part of the path to resilience. Giving yourself grace as you walk this path is key to your success. Not only is being kind to yourself important for your well-being, it is good training as you learn to express compassion for others.[30] Self-compassion is core to being a Modern Leader. As one of our students said, "It's the HEART of HEART!"

It is our deepest wish that through reading this book and putting its ideas into practice, you shut down your computer at the end of your workday with a sense of satisfaction for the impactful progress you've made. We hope that sense of satisfaction gives you a new wave of energy to cross into the rest of your day, looking forward to engaging with friends and family. And when your head hits the pillow, you rest with ease, knowing that you're OK, your family is OK, your work is OK because you have the confidence to know that even if plans didn't unfold as you expected, you have the internal resources and external support to work together to create a new plan, and it, too, will be OK. This is the heart of resiliency. You do this not for yourself alone but because the world needs your talents, your wisdom, your leadership.

Always remember, you have within you the strength, the patience, and the passion to reach for the stars to change the world.

—Harriet Tubman

Modern Leaders come prepared for change, anticipating obstacles and looking for opportunities. They model for others how to fail forward and the power of knowing when to say "enough is enough." Modern Leaders know that failure is the foundation for growth. Colleagues see the success of resilient leaders' "failing forward," which inspires and creates a desire to collaborate. The resilient leader's clarity of view—neither too pessimistic nor too optimistic—builds trust and confidence in teamwork. The power skill of resiliency enables you to more effectively build and lead teams.

Reframe

Resiliency Is a Power Skill

- Reinforces your authenticity;
- Reduces burnout for yourself and your team;
- Supports well-being;
- Increases agility and the ability to adapt to market shifts;
- Enhances your personal "brand," thereby attracting loyal followers;
- Boosts your employability;
- Enables you to stay on mission and deliver on your triple bottom-line goals.

Evolving Your Leadership

Eight Ways to Increase Your Resiliency

- Fail;
- Build in micro-resiliency moments;
- Anticipate outcomes;
- Stay in the now, and focus on things you can control;
- Get comfortable with change;
- Make peace with anxiety;
- Be grateful;
- Be kind to yourself—and others;
- Be in service to something far greater than yourself.

7

Be Transparent: It's the Foundation of Trust

TRANSPARENCY is often one of the biggest stumbling blocks for leaders as they shift from a traditional to a modern approach to leadership. We get it. What to share and how much is an ongoing challenge. Take this example: We worked for nearly a year with a fast-growing start-up company whose CEO was committed to building a high performing, highly inclusive culture. We helped our client develop programs, policies, and practices to lay the foundation for success as they ramped up and grew. A key initiative we worked on was helping the client uplevel their people analytics process and systems. One of the goals was to enable the company to be able to track hiring, retention, and promotion of diverse talent. A year in and the company had robust data to share, but when it came to sharing the data, the CEO balked.

He fretted that "if we give our employees some information, they'll want more and more." Even though the employee demographic data was on par with the industry, he worried his company would be criticized as he had seen happen to larger, more established companies such as Google and Meta when they shared their data. At the root of it all was a lack of clarity on why transparency mattered. He said, "My job as the CEO is to deliver business results. Of course, I want to do that by creating a win-ning, inclusive culture, but what does transparency have to do with it?" We shared that transparency:

Builds Employee Trust

Research has shown that when a leader takes a stand on conten-tious issues while concurrently expressing their understanding that others might have a different point of view, trust skyrock-ets for employees. Additionally, when a leader is perceived as more authentic, their employees are more likely to trust them.[1] Katy Shields, vice president of people and places at photo-app start-up and creative community VSCO, says, "My job was so much easier once I admitted that, while I have some good ideas, I don't have all of the answers. Your people are closest to the work, they're the closest to the customers, they're going to know what's best for your company. You, of course, will have context that they may not know, but they're also going to have ideas that you may not think of, so sharing needs to be part of the company culture."[2]

Increases Employee Engagement

According to TINYpulse, an employee engagement software solution, there is a direct link between employee engagement (aka "happiness") and management transparency. In fact, in their study of 40,000 employees from 150 different companies, management transparency was the top factor for employee happiness.

Increases Employee Sense of Belonging

After relationships with family and friends, our workplace is the third most important source of community, so feeling a sense of belonging at work is key to our well-being. According to the NeuroLeadership Institute, "When employees feel out of the loop, studies show, they trust managers and colleagues less, feel less company loyalty, and they are less motivated to perform. In one study, feeling out of the loop correlated with a 58% drop in perceived group standing—an employee's perception of where they rank compared to others."[3,4] In other words, you increase belonging when you are more transparent with your teams.

Improves Collaboration among Employees

Employees who feel they can trust their colleagues, who are engaged, and feel a sense of belonging are much more likely to collaborate to get work done. Stephanie Spangler, associate general counsel at McKinsey, says, "In my own experience, a successful collaboration is built on transparency and communication. Each member of the team may benefit from having visibility into the goal or the scope of the problem and also what others are doing as part of that workstream. Collaboration will likely fail if knowledge is siloed, making information sharing a key element to enable collaboration."[5]

Increases Productivity

As outlined earlier, transparency builds trust, employee engagement, and belonging—all key elements of employee happiness. And guess what. A study out of the University of Warwick showed that happier employees are 12% more productive.[6]

Delivers Bottom Line Results

IBM conducted a study of over 1,700 CEOs from 64 countries and 18 industries. Companies that outperform their peers are 30% more likely to identify openness as a key influence on their organization.[7]

Creates Trust with External Stakeholders

A meta-analysis of over 49 studies on citizens trust showed that the "overall effect of transparency on trust is positive and significant."[8]

Attracts Next-Gen Talent

Millennial and Gen Z job seekers are significantly more likely to say they want their employer to "make trustworthy information about contentious issues available to the public."[9]

And then we told our client about Ray Dalio, founder of Bridgewater Associates, an asset management firm. Eight years after starting Bridgewater, he nearly lost everything and was so financially destitute he had to borrow $4,000 from his father just to pay his family bills. In his 2017 TED Talk, Ray said, "It was one of the most painful experiences of my life, but it turned out to be one of the greatest experiences of my life because it changed my attitude to decision-making. Rather than thinking, 'I'm right,' I started to ask myself, 'How do I know I am right?' I gained a humility I needed."[10]

With this new humble mindset, Ray asked himself, "What would I do differently in the future so I won't make that same painful mistake?" He realized information flow was the fundamental issue. To make decisions, he needed radical truthfulness and radical transparency. As a leader, he needed feedback and to be willing to hear that feedback. Finally, the company needed a way to be transparent in its process so investors could regain faith in the investing process.

Ray instituted what he called "radical transparency" as a core value and embedded it into every aspect of the business from how employees interact to how the company shares its data. The result? Bridgewater Associates is now one of the biggest hedge funds in the world with over $160 billion (!) under management.

Radical transparency fosters goodness in so many ways for the same reasons that bad things are more likely to take place behind closed doors.

—Ray Dalio, founder of Bridgewater Associates[11]

European digital product design company Boldare has been using radical transparency since it started, in 2004. They use one source for all communications—in their case, Slack—and strongly discourage private messaging or back-channel conversations. Internally, they share company financial status each month, and externally, they share how they divvy up their profits: 20% to employees, 20% to shareholders, 15% to employee training and education, 10% to education and equality-based CSR initiatives.

Adam Zeimba, one of their customer success executives, explained it this way: "In its purest form, a radically transparent company has no secrets. All information is available to all employees, at all levels, regardless of individual role, responsibility or remuneration. Radical transparency means the largest number of ideas, opinions and perspectives within a company are available as a matter of course, allowing the best to be used to create success."[12]

We explained to our client that "radical transparency" may not be the answer for every leader or every company, but transparency overall helps leaders build trust with their employees so they can gather the vital information they need to lead. More knowledge and collaboration results in better, more nuanced decision-making.

But that's not the only reason for a Modern Leader to be transparent. The core reason is that in today's world, leaders don't have another choice. At its most basic, transparency is about power—the person or company with information has power over others by virtue of having that knowledge. Traditionally, companies—and the leaders who ran them—were loath to be transparent about anything that might limit their ability to drive profits. The goal was to ensure that what was communicated was in the best interests of the company—which meant, the best interests of the shareholders. As a result, companies wanted to share as little as possible.

In the past, it was often the forces of government that drove companies to be more transparent. For example, the US Civil Rights Act of 1964 launched the Equal Employment Opportunity Commission, which requires companies to report data on employee demographics. The 1970 US Environmental Protection

Act put in place requirements for companies to report on what chemicals they release into the environment. Other laws such as the Occupational Health and Safety Act require reporting on workplace conditions, and so on.

But in the 21st century, the demand for transparency has shifted from government oversight to a myriad of critical stakeholders including consumers, investors, customers, and employees.

As we move from shareholder capitalism to stakeholder capitalism where companies are being called to deliver more than just profits to shareholders and where technology has disrupted how and what information can be shared, *transparency is not an option, it's a mandate.*

Who's Demanding More Transparency?

Consumers

A recent study by public relations powerhouse Edelman revealed that 64% of consumers will buy or advocate for a brand based solely on the company's position on social or political issues. The research further revealed that 60% of consumers say brands should make it easier to see their values and positions on important issues. If they don't, these consumers will buy from someone else.[13]

Richard Edelman, president and CEO of Edelman, argues that a company that is not transparent about what it believes in and what actions it is taking to reflect those beliefs will lose sales. He says, "Brands are now being pushed to go beyond their classic business interests to become advocates. It is a new relationship between company and consumer, where purchase is premised on the brand's willingness to live its values, act with purpose, and if necessary, make the leap into activism."[14]

Investors

As we mentioned in Chapter 1, "Everything's Changed," the rise of ESG (environmental, social, and governance) investing is forcing more transparency from companies. Larry Fink, CEO of BlackRock, one of the world's largest investment management companies, says, "I'm a big believer in transparency. We are not dictating how a company goes forward, but we are asking each company to be transparent and tell us your pathway."[15]

To ensure companies are both transparent and accountable, reporting solutions such as Sustainability Accounting Standards Board (SASB)—a United States based nonprofit organization founded in 2011 to develop sustainability accounting metrics—have been created to provide third-party validation for data shared by companies. This is just one example of the external forces driving companies to be more transparent. Consider what the stock exchange Nasdaq is doing.

As of 2021, Nasdaq has placed board diversity requirements on all companies that want to be or want to remain listed on its exchange. Companies must have, or explain why they do not have, one diverse director by December 31, 2023, and two diverse directors by December 31, 2025. And, they must maintain these requirements on an ongoing basis because companies will now be required to report their board makeup yearly to Nasdaq.

Customers

The supply chain has become a hot topic for transparency. As companies commit to ESG, they in turn are forcing their suppliers to be more committed to sustainability. Jackie Sturm, corporate vice president, Supply Chain Operations at Intel, said: "Stakeholders have growing expectations of resilient and responsible supply chains across the entire product lifecycle. Our [. . .] circular economy strategies will enable Intel to reduce our environmental impact, extend product life, maximize reuse, open up new revenue streams and reduce total cost of ownership—a true 'win-win' formula."[16]

This isn't just about the climate, it is also about suppliers' employee demographics. For example, Intel will not retain or use outside law firms in the US that are average or below average on diversity. Firms are eligible to do legal work for Intel only if they meet two diversity criteria: at least 21% of the firm's US equity partners are women, and at least 10% of the firm's US equity partners are underrepresented minorities.[17]

Small and mid-sized company leaders who sell into the enterprise market with clients such as Microsoft, Meta, Oracle, Bank of America, and many of the other large companies are often stumped when faced with these new requirements. Never before have they had to look honestly at their leadership teams or their workplace cultures to make the sale. Now, everything has changed, and they are being forced to share employee demographics in order to compete to win business.

The CEO of an office supply company, a client of PrismWork, was blindsided when he received a request for proposal (RFP) from Meta, one of his biggest and longest-standing customers. When he asked his client why the new rules, he was told, "The world has changed and we want to keep up with these changes. We expect our suppliers to do the same."

Employees

Research has shown again and again that today's employees want to work for companies that reflect their values. For example, a 2022 survey by Qualtrics revealed that more than half of US employees—54%—said they would be willing to take a pay cut to work at a company that shares their values. And 56% said they wouldn't even consider a job at a company that has values they disagree with.[18]

How do you convey your values? It's about, you guessed it, transparency, and you better be walking the talk. If you say your value is fostering an inclusive culture, you can be sure your current and future employees will hold you to it.

A 2021 study of job seekers done by Glassdoor, a job search website, revealed that 76% consider a company's workforce diversity when they evaluate a job opportunity. As a result,

Glassdoor gives this advice to companies: "Remember that your employees are a significant part of your employer brand. Candidates are looking for signs of diversity on your site and in your online profiles, but they will also talk to their friends and read reviews on Glassdoor to find out how diverse a company actually is."[19] In other words, you can't hide because there are more ways than ever for potential employees to find out the truth about your company.

Employee demographic data is one area where companies are feeling pressure; another key transparency issue for companies is pay equity. As of January 2023, 42 U.S. states have passed pay transparency laws requiring employers to disclose information about employee compensation, either to the employees themselves or to the public. Depending on the jurisdiction, these laws require employers to:

- Provide applicants the salary range for a posted position at a specified point during the hiring process;
- Provide employees salary range upon request, when changing jobs, or upon hire;
- Include salary range in job postings.

One of the challenges with pay transparency is that even when a company is transparent, many employees still don't believe it. A 2022 study by Payscale of over 33,000 knowledge workers showed 86% of people who were paid above market, still believed they were paid at market or below, and 57% of those being paid at market believed they were being paid below the market. The study also found that higher pay transparency decreases likelihood that employees will seek a new job, painting a clear picture for what organizations can do to reduce turnover and increase retention.[20]

Modern Leaders know that transparency around employee demographic data and pay are essential for attracting and retaining top talent today.

You Need to Know

Salary Reveal Parties: Allyship and the Next Wave of Transparency

Just in case you don't think transparency around pay equity is an issue for you, consider what happened to a senior executive at a global financial services firm in charge of a large marketing division. One night, a group of 10 marketing colleagues who reported into her division decided to host a "Salary Reveal Party." It started when one of the men in the group was skeptical that pay equity was an issue at their company. He dismissed the possibility that his female coworkers could be paid less than he and the other three men on the team.

So the six women and four men gathered for dinner at a local restaurant. Each had a note card, and on it they wrote their base pay, their signing bonus, and their annual bonus. Count down to one, two, three—and each flipped over their card revealing their compensation. To no woman's surprise, each of the men made more than they did.

"How could this be?" the skeptic cried in incredulous disbelief. "Most of the women on our team have more experience than me, and I was hired after three of you. It's not right!"

The women agreed; then the men acted. They went in to the senior executive and complained. They also posted a complaint to human resources. The good news is their complaints were heard. The company launched an internal pay equity analysis and were dismayed to learn there was a pervasive problem across a number of departments. They have since made adjustments and have publicly committed to pay equity.

The Covid-19 pandemic presented a perfect case study of how transparency can help support company culture and reinforce company values. The MIT *Sloan Management Review //* Glassdoor Culture 500 is the largest systematic study of corporate culture ever conducted. It is an ongoing analysis of over 1.4 million employee written reviews on Glassdoor that tracks employee sentiment over time. A key finding before and during Covid showed that employees' perception of their company culture skyrocketed during Covid Why? Transparent communications. The ongoing study revealed that how companies and their leaders communicated emerged as *the* most important differentiator between companies that saw a significant boost in their culture values score and those that suffered a sharp decline.[21]

Other research of over 400 HR leaders asked open-ended questions about the most meaningful thing their organization did to support the transition to remote work during Covid-19. "High-quality communication" was the top answer, mentioned by nearly half of all respondents.[22] In other words, what and how leaders and companies shared made all the difference when it came to employee engagement and satisfaction in the greatest disruption to work in this century.

So, as we told our start-up client, you can do what Traditional Leaders used to do and wait until the government puts the screws on or be blindsided by a consumer boycott or be unable to hire and retain diverse talent all because you refuse

You can't be a Modern Leader without embracing transparency as a core value and building it as a core competency.

to be open and honest about how you run your business. Or you can do what Modern Leaders do and put transparency at the center of your approach to leadership and as a foundation of your business strategy.

The Five Core Attributes of Transparency

When it comes to transparency, Modern Leaders exhibit the five following attributes. They:

1) Know Where They Stand

Modern Leaders are clear for themselves and make clear to others their values and priorities, what they will and will not accommodate.

2) Have The Courage To Stand In Their Why

Modern Leaders have the courage to stand in their why even if it means they risk being canceled on social media. They know standing in their why makes them predictable to others. It provides consistency to decisions and provides a foundation to explain their choices.

3) Communicate with Candor

Modern Leaders communicate with candor. When they see something, they say something—congratulations or corrections. They give constructive feedback to their employees and are authentic in their messaging when dealing with the big events.

4) Seek Feedback and Act on it

Modern Leaders know transparency is a two-way street. They understand that when they're more transparent with their team, they can expect more direct and transparent communication from their team. When leaders seek feedback, they disclose it and share their action plan for development. They welcome and respond positively to honest feedback, which promotes a culture of resilience and humility.

5) Are Humble and Accessible

Like Ray Dalio, Modern Leaders are humble and make themselves available so they can truly hear what they need to make smart decisions. They leverage their humility to show vulnerability. As renowned executive coach Allison Elvekrog often says, "Vulnerability is human Velcro."

The key to building transparency as a power skill is understanding that transparency is about trust. Modern Leaders must operate with the understanding that transparency is essential to building trust across your organization and beyond.

> *I believe a culture of trust today is more essential than it's ever been. With digital technology we basically have full transparency to information. And there's a higher expectation amongst individuals to know, to be included, to basically be part of the conversation. As leaders today, more than ever, we need to have transparency to build trust in the organizations we lead.*
>
> **—Andrew Swinand, CEO,**
> **Leo Burnett North America**[23]

Brian Chesky, CEO of Airbnb, provided a MasterClass on how to use transparency as a power skill with his memo to employees in May 2020, announcing the difficult layoffs as the pandemic travel restrictions devastated the business. He begins his note by taking accountability for past communications. "When you've asked me about layoffs, I've said that nothing is off the table." And continues with, "Let me start with how we arrived at this decision." Brian closes the note by sharing the principles, guided by the company's core values, for their approach to the reductions in their workforce. He shows the courage to stand in his why: "I have done my best to stay true to these principles." The communication goes on to outline what will happen next for those departing and those staying, and he finishes with a personal account: "I have a deep feeling of love for all of you.

Our mission is not merely about travel. When we started Airbnb, our original tagline was, 'Travel like a human.' The human part was always more important than the travel part. What we are about is belonging."[25]

You Need to Know

The Link between Transparency and Trust

In their outstanding book *Unleashed: The Unapologetic Leader's Guide to Empowering Everyone Around You*, Harvard Business School Professor Francis Frei and Anne Morriss, executive director of the Leadership Consortium, argue that leadership in today's world must be founded on trust, and transparency is what builds trust. They write, "People don't always realize how the information (or more often, the misinformation) that they're broadcasting may undermine their own trustworthiness."[24]

Based on extensive research, Francis and Anne have determined that trust is built on three things: authenticity, logic, and empathy. As they have defined it, authenticity means that people believe they are interacting with the real you, logic means they have faith in your judgment and competence, and empathy is when they feel you care about them and are invested in their success:

Authenticity—I experience the real you;

Logic—I know you can do it; your reasoning and judgment are sound; and

Empathy—I believe you care about me and my success.

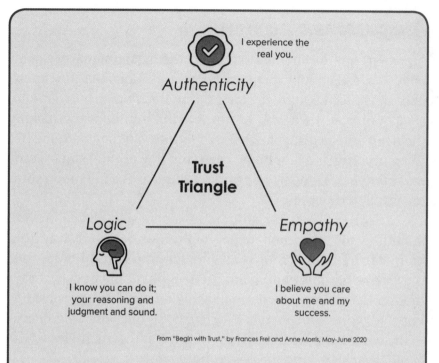

I experience the
real you.

Authenticity

**Trust
Triangle**

Logic ———————— *Empathy*

I know you can do it;
your reasoning and
judgment and sound.

I believe you care
about me and my
success.

From "Begin with Trust," by Frances Frei and Anne Morris, May-June 2020

Transparency becomes essential in this paradigm because if you say one thing and do another, you send mixed messages that undermine at least one if not more core elements of trust. It's a way of walking your talk, consistently expressing your values, and ensuring that your actions align with those values.

Brian received accolades from employees and the press for his transparency. Despite the layoffs, Brian's transparency also won shareholders when the company went public just nine months later. The company is now worth $71 billion and counting. Why? In part because Brian's transparency built trust across his key stakeholders.

Modern Leaders commit to transparency because they know it is core to building trust with employees, consumers, and communities around the world.

Transparency and Your Team

Transparency doesn't just happen in the big moments of a company. It's also about everyday interactions. Consider the experience of Jessica Leonard, a rising star in the finance industry.

Not only is she a whiz at running the numbers and making the deals, she is also a huge fan of tattoos. So much so, she has them over much of her body. Leafs and flowers and stars, words and numbers, a girl swinging from a large tree, a full moon shining through its leaves.

Each one of Jessica's tattoos represents a significant life event including one in memory of her nephew who passed away from brain cancer at only four years old. Jessica is proud of her ink, they make her feel confident and beautiful, but she has always hidden her tattoos at work. She worried she'd be perceived as unprofessional and not taken seriously, so she wore long sleeves in the winter and refrained from tatting her legs or ankles so she could wear skirts and dresses without worry.

When she landed her dream job as a partner at Evolution Capital, a small-business private equity firm in Cleveland, and was asked to update her professional photo, Jessica decided to come clean.

Jessica shared what happened next on a LinkedIn post that went viral and landed her, and her boss, in national news. She wrote, "I was cautious but asked our Managing Partner if he was comfortable with me getting a photo taken sans jacket for my personal use on LinkedIn, but that we'd use one with the jacket for our website."

His response—"Let's roll with the tattoos in both! Loud and proud!"[26]

Jessica's boss, Jeffery Kadlic, explained to *Good Morning America*, "It is the content of one's character that is most important to us. Authenticity and transparency are cornerstones of the culture we are working to create. We see Jess for who she is and embrace all of her because she shares our core values and is a tremendous talent. At the end of the day, that is all that really matters."[27]

Jessica closed her LinkedIn post with this: "Sometimes, you come across those leaders who not only allow you to show up every day as you are, but they also expect it. Those leaders who have recognized that whether I'm in the jacket or not, I'm the same person, the same business professional . . . a female leader who will most certainly be taken seriously."[28]

Boom!

Jeffery Kadlic is a great example of a Modern Leader who understands that supporting his employees to be authentic each and every day fosters trust, inclusion, and belonging.

Transparency, Authenticity, and Code Switching

As a leader, it is important to remember that your employees and colleagues may not feel safe or comfortable being transparent and fully authentic. They may feel they have to hide pieces of themselves in order to fit into the majority culture. Tricia Montalvo Timm knows this only too well. She is a first-generation Latina, the daughter of immigrant parents—her mother from El Salvador, her father from Ecuador. Because Tricia is light-skinned and fair-haired, she can pass as white, and she did for the first four decades of her life.

Born in Los Angeles, Tricia and her family were the only people of color in their neighborhood. She went to a majority white high school, then on to college (the first in her family to have done so), and finally on to law school. She excelled in each of these places, captain of this, head of that, graduating cum laude and landing her first job at a prestigious law firm in Silicon Valley. In each of these places she hid her identity for fear that showing up as Latina would limit her opportunities, "As I started each new chapter of my life, I kept conformity as my guiding principle," Tricia writes in her book *Embrace the Power of You: Owning Your Identity at Work*. "I didn't wake up one day and say,

'I am going to downplay my ethnicity today!' It was something I learned over time. All of the messages I had heard growing up gave me the feeling that my ethnicity would not be valued. I did not want to take the risk that it could jeopardize my career or my social status."

Like many people who are "different"—for example, immigrants, members of the LGBTQ+ community, people of color, those who practice a non-majority religion, mothers, the list goes on—Tricia learned to "code switch." This means she adapted her behavior, her style of speech, and her appearance to conform to the prevailing culture's norm, and this hiding worked for Tricia, but it came at deep personal cost.

In less than 10 years, she succeeded in becoming general counsel for a high-flying software company. But the toll of hiding became unbearable. In her book, Tricia recounts the many times she sat in silence as a colleague, a parent on her kids soccer team, a boss made jokes or said something disparaging about Latinos. She stewed, she steamed, and she worried she didn't deserve all of her success. Eventually, the pressure became too great, and Tricia suffered an emotional break. With counseling and support from her family and friends, Tricia took steps to be authentic.

At her book launch event in February 2023, Tricia shared, "My imposter syndrome was real. Despite all of my hard work, I didn't believe I deserved that seat at the table. It took years for me to unpack the lessons I had learned, but once I did, the world opened up to me in ways I could never have imagined." Tricia—who had always showed up as Tricia Timm—decided it was time to reclaim her identity. She stopped straightening her hair, added her maiden name, Montalvo, to her LinkedIn page, and began posting about her Latina heritage. She also landed the role of general counsel at tech start-up Looker. The stress of hiding was gone, and for the first time she felt she could bring her full self to work. "It was liberating," she told the rapt audience. It was also rewarding. Looker was sold to Google for $2.6 billion, and now Tricia Montalvo Timm commits her time to supporting other Latinas and sharing her story. "I now see that living my truth helps others to live in theirs. My life is better than I could ever imagine. I want every person to be able to feel confident in who they are and own their full identity at work and in all areas of their lives."

We're told to "bring our whole selves to work," but as you can see from Tricia's story, it's not that easy. A Modern Leader understands this and does her or his best to create safe spaces for their employees and colleagues.

Which brings us back to our client. With these insights, our client understood that transparency is a key business driver for Modern Leaders. We are working with him now to design an internal and external messaging campaign around all that they are doing to foster a winning, inclusive culture. We know this will set his company up for success when they are ready to go public in the not-too-distant future.

Reframe

Transparency Is a Power Skill

- Builds trust with all stakeholders;
- Promotes a sense of fairness;
- Creates safe spaces for employees;
- Increases collaboration;
- Fosters inclusion and belonging;
- Enhances employee engagement and productivity;
- Attracts next-generation talent;
- Reinforces a leader's and a company's values.

Evolving Your Leadership

Three Steps To Increase Your Transparency

Leaders often struggle with what and how to communicate. These prompts are intended to help you deliver more transparent communication:

1) Start With Why

    "Here's why this matters."

    "Here's what I think."

2) Move To What

    "Here's what we know for sure."

    "Here's what we don't know."

3) Get To How

    "Here's what you can count on from me."

    "Here's what you can do."

Adapted from Peter Meyers and Shann Nix, *As We Speak: How to Make Your Point and Have It Stick*, Atria, 2011.

8

Be Inclusive: It's a Win for All

EACH time Lisen and JeanAnn teach about inclusivity, we ask the students, "So what do you think two white, straight, cis-gender, married moms who live in suburbia have to do with diversity, equity, inclusion, and belonging?"

The truth is, they aren't sure. Our answer: "Everything!"

It doesn't matter if you are white, gay, straight, rich, poor, young, old, able-bodied, Black, immigrant, female, male, parent, single, Latine, trans, a CEO, or a first-time manager, you cannot be a leader in today's workplace without being 100% committed to hiring and retaining diverse teams of talent, ensuring equity—particularly pay equity—is embedded in your organization's programs and policies, and doing everything in your power to foster inclusive cultures where the rainbow of your employees feel seen, connected, supported, and proud to work for you. This is not a rant; this is a truth.

We're not here to say it's easy. In fact, it is one of the most challenging aspects of being a leader today. But it is essential if you are committed to having triple bottom-line impact. One of the key problems is that when someone starts talking about diversity or equity or inclusion or even belonging, many leaders start to zone out. Perhaps they think, "This isn't about me"

> **As a Modern Leader, your success, the success of your team, and the success of your company depends on inclusivity. Full. Stop.**

or "This is a waste of time." Or they aren't directly connecting it to the bottom line. Or, if they're more honest with themselves, they realize they feel blamed or shamed or discomforted in some way. Or, as our research has shown, they just don't know how to be an inclusive leader. We get it. But we want to be clear, inclusivity is foundational to Modern Leadership.

What do we mean by that? We mean Modern Leaders understand and value that we each come with unique experiences and skills and insights. We mean that we are all much more than a demographic: none of us is one thing. We have identities that are intersectional and complex. And these combined experiences, and skills and identities, are the source of your company's innovation and competitive edge. This is why Modern Leaders put diversity, equity, inclusion, and belonging (DEIB) at the center of their triple bottom-line approach to business.

Inclusivity is Good For Business

It used to be that we had to prove to our clients that diversity was foundational for business success. However, our recent experience and research shows that isn't the case anymore—even for white, straight, middle-aged men. Before we go on, if that describes you, we're not trying to call you out or blame and shame you, we're just acknowledging the meta-narrative that men who fit that mold have been perceived as being resistant to DEIB.

But we know that is no longer true.

How do we know this? In 2022, PrismWork conducted a landmark study, the Men@Work Research Initiative, with the support of the W.K. Kellogg Foundation. We surveyed, interviewed, and hosted small group roundtables with over 2,400 college educated men across the United States. The vast majority were married (79%) and fathers (70%). Among the partnered men, most were primary breadwinners in their households (71%). The men in our study were primarily between the ages of 35 and 50 (61%) and in middle to upper-middle management (60%).

These men are what other researchers have called the "frozen middle"—that crucial center of the organization tasked with the day-to-day realities of delivering on companies' objectives. If companies truly want to foster inclusive cultures that deliver on the bottom-line promise of DEIB, the day-to-day responsibility lies with these men.

When it comes to buying into the power and importance of DEIB in the workplace, here's the good news:

- **78%** of men agree that managing a diverse team makes them a better leader.
- **74%** believe that diverse teams lead to better business outcomes.
- **66%** believe that DEIB is foundational to a company's success.

In other words, those who have historically been perceived as most resistant to the concept of diversity, equity, inclusion, and belonging are finally converts. This is a sea change in the workplace and, we believe, a huge opportunity for senior leaders—in fact, leaders at every level—to create and foster sustainable cultures that deliver impact for all stakeholders.

Our research validated that those men who are most engaged as inclusive leaders are the most equipped to lead in today's complex work environments:

- **1.3x** more confident in their ability to support and champion their employees;
- **1.4x** more committed to fostering real culture change within their company;

- **1.4x** more likely to approach leadership with a "we" mindset;
- **1.5x** more likely to mentor/sponsor/hire diverse talent.

In other words, men who approach their roles as leaders with inclusivity at their core are exactly the leaders every company wants and needs. However, just in case someone you work with is still harboring doubts about the value of DEIB, here are a few additional stats to reinforce the dollars and sense:

- Companies with executive teams that include at least one female are 48% more likely to financially outperform those without any women (on EBIT, earnings before interest and taxes).[1] And the more gender homogeneous the executive team, the more likely they were to *underperform* relative to diverse teams.[2]
- Companies with one or more women board members had higher average return on investment (ROI) and better average growth than companies with male only boards.[3,4]
- Companies with above average diversity produced a greater proportion of revenue from innovation (45% of total) than companies with below average diversity (26%).[5]
- For start-ups, those with at least one female or non-white founder deliver 30% higher multiple on invested capital.[6]
- Research from Stanford University's Margaret Neale shows causation that having more women on a board leads to better performance, as stock price increases followed diversity announcements.
- High belonging was linked to a whopping 56% increase in job performance, a 50% drop in turnover risk, and a 75% reduction in sick days. For a 10,000-person company, this would result in annual savings of more than $52M.[7]

We could go on—and on and on—but we're pretty sure you get it.

The 21st century workplace requires leaders who can manage and inspire today's increasingly diverse workforce. Those who are committed and engaged in DE&I are the very leaders companies need to succeed in today's complex environment.

—**Antonio Lucio, principal and founder, 5S Diversity; former global chief marketing officer HP, Meta, and Visa**

DEIB: Some Definitions for Clarity

In business today, there are a number of words floating around that can lead to confusion and, as we mentioned earlier, discomfort for some. So let's get clear on what we mean when we say diversity, equity, inclusion, and belonging.

In 2016, renowned inclusion advocate and Harvard-trained lawyer Verna Myers was giving a talk to the Cleveland Bar Association. She explained to the audience that in 1953 when Harvard Law School finally admitted its first female students, the women quickly discovered that the Ivy League school had not provided any bathrooms for them.

"So what's the message?" Myers asked the crowd. "Don't stay long," came the answer from someone in the back. She laughed, agreed, and explained that embracing inclusion at work requires "the institution's ability to fully integrate its understanding of and appreciation for the diverse cultures and backgrounds of its employees."

Then Myers went on to give her now famous quote: "Diversity is about being invited to the party; inclusion is about getting asked to dance."[8]

At PrismWork, we've taken her concept two steps further (yes, pun intended).

Diversity

Diversity is about representation. It is quantifiable and trackable. It's about data. The Equal Employment Opportunity Commission (EEOC) requires companies with 100 or more employees to track and report race/ethnicity and gender identities on an annual basis. This is the baseline of diversity. For companies, and unfortunately many leaders, it is often focused on hiring (getting as many people who meet the EEOC requirements in the door as possible) without true attention to fostering cultures where the diverse talent want to stay.

Equity

Equity is about fairness. Do we have access to the same opportunities, are we paid equitably, are similar professional development opportunities spread fairly across the organization? A company might have a diverse workforce overall and meet some EEOC data requirements but may not have any women or people of color in senior management. Or an organization may seemingly have an inclusive culture, but pay and benefits favor men over women. Like diversity, equity is typically data driven, can be tracked, and can be a source of insight into solutions. For example, organizations struggling to retain and promote diverse candidates may need to be more proactive about investing in training, mentoring, or networking connections for historically marginalized groups to help them have a more equitable chance at getting promoted.

Inclusion

Inclusion is about being invited to get involved. It's the process of creating a working culture and environment that recognizes, appreciates, and effectively utilizes the talents, skills, and perspectives of every employee. The dictionary definition is: the state of being taken in as part of a whole. But it is still majority focused. The employer or manager or majority community gets to decide if an employee is worthy of being included, and this is often why inclusion efforts fail.

"Bring your full self to work" has been a mantra of inclusion efforts in recent years, but the truth in most situations is that employees often feel they can't show up as their full selves because they aren't part of the majority culture and so do not feel fully welcomed. A Deloitte study of more than 3,000 people found that 61% of people hide at least one dimension of themselves in the workplace. More so if they are Black (79%) or gay (83%).[9] This is where belonging enters the party.

Belonging

Belonging is the focus of best-in-class workplace cultures. This is emotion focused, and it's employee-centric, not employer-centric. This is about how the employee feels. Remember Jessica Leonard? Her boss, Jeffery Kadlic, encouraged her to be authentic and transparent. But lots of bosses say this but don't mean it—he acted on it and supported her tattooed self. The result? Jessica felt like she belonged at her new company. Jeffrey couldn't force or mandate how Jessica felt, but he was able to behave in a way that supported it. Modern Leaders must understand that belonging is not about them, it's about how their employees feel in response to the culture and values of the organization.

Diversity:
"Getting invited to the dance"
- Representation
- Head
- Focus on hiring
- Employer-centric

Equity:
"Getting access to the dance"
- Fairness
- Head
- Focus on promotion
- Employer-centric

Inclusion:
"Giving input to the playlist"
- Involvement
- Head
- Focus on Retention
- Employer-centric

Belonging:
"Dancing without a care in the world"
- Engagement
- Heart
- Focus on business outcomes
- Employee-centric

A 2020 national survey of nearly 4,000 college educated professionals revealed the power of belonging. The research showed that professionals in the highest quartile of belonging scores are far more likely than those in the lowest to say they are very engaged at work (97% vs. 54%), very loyal to their organization (93% vs. 35%), intend to stay at least two years (88% vs. 61%), and would recommend their company as a good place to work (71% vs. 17%).[10] Additionally, BetterUp research shows employees who feel they belong take 75% fewer sick days.[11] This means more team members come to work and are more productive at work. Obviously, a more engaged, productive workforce is essential to a company's bottom line.

Coqual, a research organization focused on DEIB, has mapped out the core elements of belonging as feeling seen, connected, supported, and proud. Miss on one of these elements, and you miss on belonging.

You Need to Know

The Top Four Things Employees Need to Feel They Belong

1) To Be **Seen**
   - Feeling their contributions are valued;
   - Being recognized for their contributions.

2) To Feel **Connected**
   - Feeling comfortable to be themselves at work;
   - Feeling like their team cares about them as a person.

3) To Feel **Supported**
   - Having the opportunity to express their opinions freely;
   - Getting feedback on their personal and professional development.

4) To Be **Proud**
   - Feeling aligned with the values and purpose of the organization;
   - Having confidence the company is walking the talk when it comes to their commitments to people and the planet.

Adapted from "The Power of Belonging: What It Is and Why It Matters in Today's Workplace," by Coqual, June 2020.

DEIB—It's Nuanced

In October of 2022, EY conducted a study of over 3,000 full-time professionals working at large enterprise organizations, those that are most likely to have structured DEIB programs and initiatives. Two years after the death of George Floyd and the dramatic rise of commitments by companies to DEIB, they wanted the employee experience and attitudes around diversity and inclusion. What did they learn? It's nuanced.

"The workforce isn't a monolithic group, and organizations need to stay abreast of their people's expectations around DE&I," said Leslie Patterson, EY Americas and US diversity, equity, and inclusiveness leader.

The study revealed each demographic group viewed DEIB differently. For example, Gen Z workers said they associated DEIB with a commitment to community support through corporate responsibility efforts and volunteering (44%) as well as through the establishment of employee resource groups (34%). Three out of four millennials (76%) said they are willing to leave their employer if DEIB initiatives were not offered.

For the majority of Black employees (57%), DEIB is about a company's investment in the development and advancement of underrepresented populations at work. LGBTQ respondents believed DEIB equates to a culture that focuses on belonging (53%).

When we teach our class of next-gen leaders, we make sure our students understand that DEIB is more than a check-the-box activity. Lisen has shared with our students, "I'm a mother, an older woman, a writer by avocation, and I am neurodiverse. You might be a younger Black man who is an engineer by training and has no children. I might approach the world as right-brained creative, and you might bring your left-brain analytical skills to our collaborations. These unique, intersectional differences aren't captured on EEOC forms, but this is true diversity, and it is much harder to track. So it is incumbent on a leader to understand that box checking is not the answer to diversity. It's about being sure that when you look around that proverbial table, that you have a diversity of age and experience, diversity of skill, diversity of economic background, diversity of gender identity, diversity of ethnic and racial identity, and, most importantly, diversity of thought."

Inclusive Leadership: A Modern Model

Kai Deveraux Lawson, senior vice president, Diversity, Equity & Inclusion at a global advertising agency, is a regular guest executive to our class. In the winter of 2022, she shared how she became a committed DEIB advocate and leader. It started with her own experiences with belonging in the workplace: "I distinctly remember one moment during my first couple of months in advertising where it was the BET Awards and Beyoncé was performing, and that's all I wanted to talk about the next day. And nobody gave a damn that Beyoncé performed at the BET Awards. Beyoncé! I thought to myself, 'Oh, shit, I'm alone. I'm actually going to just have to be excited all by myself'." In that moment, Kai didn't feel connected or supported by her colleagues; she felt like an outsider.

Kai didn't plan on having a career as a diversity champion, but she says, "It was micro-moments like that where I started to recognize that there's a culture in this industry that's a little bit different from the culture that I represent and that I'm used to representing." To bring sunlight to the challenging issues of being "othered" in the workplace, Kai partnered with two colleagues of color to launch *The Mixed Company* podcast, an award-winning truth-telling platform with the tagline, "Making uncomfortable conversations comfortable one episode at a time."

"It was a way to speak truth to power and bring solutions to the table," she said. Kai has continued to do that and, as a result, her career has flourished. Not only does she champion change internally at her agency, she works closely with their clients to help their cultures be more inclusive.

Kai says this is what gives her hope: "For the first time in my career, I am finally seeing brands who understand that how they are on the inside is as important as how they show up to the outside world."

Kai is the model of an inclusive leader—she understands her why, works with her company's system to make change for others, and she actively looks beyond the walls of her company to create impact.

Not all of us have to dedicate our careers to becoming diversity advocates, but Modern Leaders know that embedding DEIB into their programs, policies, and practices is critical for their own success, the success of their teams and company, and for the success of previously underrepresented talent ready to impact the triple bottom line.

You Need to Know

The "I" in the HEARTI model draws on all the Modern Leader power skills. You can't be an inclusive leader without the heart of HEARTI.

- Having a servant leader mindset.
- Listening with humility and empathy.
- Holding yourself and others accountable.
- Being transparent about your goals, your wins, and your mistakes.
- Learning from the inevitable failures and having the resiliency to do it differently and better next time.
- Inclusive leaders understand that DEIB is a journey, and there is no one right path.

Inclusive Leadership: It's a Journey

Six men, leaders at their respective companies, sat in a circle around a table in the backyard of a senior vice president at

Salesforce. He had volunteered to host and participate in this gathering so we could better understand the experiences of male leaders in today's complex workplace. It was part of our Men@ Work Research Initiative.

As they went around the table, each man shared how he reacted to and approached inclusion. They were honest and vulnerable, particularly when discussing the horrific murder of George Floyd, a Black man killed by police officers in Minneapolis in May 2020. For most of these men, all of whom are white, this was the first time they had been exposed to the realities of what it means to be Black in the United States. Each of these leaders expressed regret and embarrassment at their ignorance. "I have lots of diversity on my staff. And yet, I really wasn't even aware of what they are dealing with on a daily basis," said one man. He went on to share that he has since done his best to get informed and become an advocate for people of color at his company. "I even became an executive sponsor of our multicultural ERG [employee resource group]," he announced.

DEIB Jennifer Brown writes in her must-read book, *How to Be An Inclusive Leader: Your Role in Creating Cultures of Belonging Where Everyone Can Thrive*, "Although some of us embody a mindset in which we're constantly immersed in thoughts of fairness, privilege, equality and advocacy, others are only vaguely aware of these topics on a daily basis—or are not aware of them at all." She goes on to write, "No matter where we start, as leaders we all have a responsibility to learn how to improve our knowledge, skills, and competencies to better support our colleagues, companies, and the people around us."[12]

Remember that each person wants nothing more than to be seen, heard, and valued for their unique humanity.

—Gena Cox, PhD, author of *Leading Inclusion: Drive Change Your Employees Can See and Feel*[13]

Moving from Unaware to Collaborator

Jennifer created the *Inclusive Leader Continuum* to map out how a leader can move from "unaware" to "advocate." The continuum starts with those leaders who believe it is someone else's problem to those who are proactively confronting discrimination and actively working to bring about systemic change. At PrismWork, we've updated and expanded Jennifer's continuum based on the results of our recent research and our leadership transformation work with a multitude of clients across numerous industries around the globe. We call it the *Arc of Allyship in Action*.

We see five steps on the continuum of allyship from "unaware" (those who struggle to understand or recognize the underlying issues) to "collaborator" (those leaders dedicated to triple bottom-line impact and who, as a result, use their power and privilege to routinely and proactively champion inclusion within their companies and in the world at large).

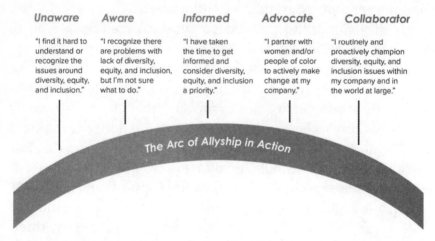

The first goal on your allyship journey is to move from recognition to action. The second goal is to move from action to impact. Modern Leaders understand that focusing on DEIB internally at their own companies is not enough. Doing so might change the culture at a given company, but it doesn't create sustainable change in the world at large. Collaborators are committed to creating systemic change, which supports all stakeholders, not just those within the proverbial four walls of their organization.

So What's Holding You Back?

What keeps leaders from becoming true collaborators? There can be many issues, but below are five internal and external forces that we see again and again in our consulting and research.

1) Implicit Bias

Neuroscientist Dr. Pragya Agarwal says that no one is immune to bias, *and* most importantly, bias can be unlearned. In her book *Sway: Unraveling Unconscious Bias,* she explains that our unconscious brain processes 11 million bits of information every second, but our conscious brain can only process 40–50 bits of information per second. As a result, our brains create a sorting system to help us manage the input, a way to categorize all of that data so we can assess risk and reward.

Here's an example: In less than one-tenth of a second, our brain categorizes people by race and gender. And what do we do with that? Using data from our life experience to determine our perceptions and attitudes, we unconsciously make decisions about people. The social constructs we have learned through our lifetimes informs our decisions. Consider the longitudinal insights from the Harvard Implicit Bias Test, which has been tracking people's biases since 1998. In all of that time, the test has shown that regardless of their own gender identity, three out of four respondents associate men with career and women with family. And three out of four respondents show a positive bias toward white people, regardless of the respondent's race or ethnicity. In other words, unconscious biases are socially con-structed reactions based on a lifetime of processing data through specific filters based on our worldview, experiences, and the social norms of the space and time we live in.

Now, this isn't an excuse for being sexist or racist or whatever -ist you want to come with, but it is an opportunity to be curious and humble. Gaining awareness of those implicit biases you have and what may be driving them can help you on your inclusive leader journey.

2) Zero-Sum Thinking

In their book *Good Guys: How Men Can Be Better Allies for Women at Work*, PrismWork collaborators and coauthors of the Men@ Work research professors Brad Johnson and David Smith, write,

> Zero-sum thinking is one of the many stumbling blocks for diversity and inclusion efforts.

Zero-sum thinking is part of a Traditional Leadership dynamic that focuses on individual success at the expense of others and competition over collaboration. This skewed perception can result in a "me vs. them" attitude that makes some leaders less motivated to collaborate with others because they feel it hurts their own chances for advancement.

One of the many challenges of zero-sum thinking is that it reinforces current workplace inequities. Our research has shown that the structures that may have previously worked for white, straight men (i.e. the ideal worker construct, the notion that success is an individual sport, etc.) no longer work. This is evidenced by men reporting high rates of burnout, frustration, and despair from new demands such as trying to balance work and family commitments, as well as confusion over what it means to lead in today's complex world. The new norms of equal participation by men and women lead some men to react by believing there is no "pie" left for them.

Zero-sum thinking can create unnecessary division, fear, and resentment. In our research, this mindset was pervasive, particularly among white men. They were nearly two times more likely than men of color to report that men are losing roles to women and similarly two times more likely to report that white men have fewer opportunities.

You Need to Know

A Special Message for Men: We Need You!

Despite significant workplace gains for women and other underrepresented groups over the past decade, men still largely hold the majority of positions of power. As a result, men are uniquely positioned to be catalysts for change in the workplace and beyond. This was the inspiration for PrismWork's 2022 landmark study on men at work.[14] When it came to supporting women at work, we learned:

- **71%** of men say that women have contributed to their success in business.
- **61%** believe the workplace is harder for women.

But when it comes to using their power and privilege to help change the system so all can thrive, most men aren't stepping up. Only **one in three** men report actively mentoring a woman.

- **40%** told us they are uncomfortable giving women critical feedback—an essential element of professional development.
- **47%** of men choose not to meet with women in private because they are afraid they will be falsely accused of a #MeToo incident.
- **58%** agreed that the #MeToo movement has impacted the professional working relationships between men and women.

It is important for men to understand that uplifting and empowering women and other diverse talent in the workplace will also allow for their load to be lighter. When we acknowledge that gender and racial bias is real and when we work together to dismantle it, it is a net positive for everyone. This is especially important for senior level executives to understand.

—Joan C. Williams, Sullivan Professor of Law and founding director of the Center for WorkLife Law at the University of California Law, San Francisco

3) Unchecked Privilege

We do a group activity in our class called "The Wheel of Power and Privilege." It's adapted from anti-oppression work done by the Canadian Council for Refugees and Canadian educator Sylvia Duckworth. In the center of the wheel is the word "power," and on the outside of the wheel is the word "marginalized."[15] Around the wheel are categories including body size, mental health, neurodiversity, immigration status, sexuality, skin color, and more. We show our students this multidimensional wheel and ask them to diagram themselves. The closer they are to the center of the wheel, the more power and privilege they have.

We define privilege as a systematically unearned advantage, in the form of resources or power, or simply by belonging to a dominant group. Think of your privilege as an invisible backpack of opportunity and social capital. This conversation is not about shame or judgment. We recognize it's uncomfortable to expose unearned advantages that have given you benefits. And we recognize that there are many other vectors that can be added to this wheel—age, location, political affiliation, religion, etc.

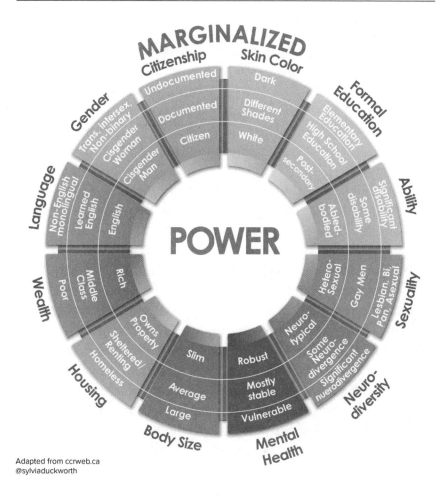

Adapted from ccrweb.ca
@sylviaduckworth

This activity is often an eye-opener for our students. For many, particularly those who have a passionate belief in meritocracy, the wheel offers a chance to reexamine that belief system and consider what they were born into and what they have chosen in their life journey.

Others realize that some measures of power and privilege are under our control and often contextual. For example, one of our students who is originally from Brazil but who currently lives and works in the United States recognized that she has less power and privilege in the US than she does when she is back in her home country. "I am Latina, have an accent when I speak English, and am not a US citizen, but when I'm in Brazil, I am part of the majority culture so my power and privilege is different in these contexts."

Other students have recognized the many ways we can't control where we land on the wheel. As one student shared, "I can't control that I have dark skin, am neurodiverse, and was born into poverty."

Not only can the Wheel of Power and Privilege educate by helping us see where we have agency and those things we truly cannot change, it also enables us to view our colleagues with deeper empathy. Those who appear as though they might be at the center of the wheel often have hidden truths. They may have grown up in an economically disadvantaged household suffering from food scarcity, they may struggle with neurodiversity, they may be gay or lesbian and unable to be out and proud because of the culture in which they were raised or currently live. Point being, Modern Leaders understand that we can't assume we know other people's lived realities, that pathways to success may be far longer for some than others, and that our job as leaders is to bring our humility, curiosity, courage, and growth mindset to our interactions with others.

4) Lack of Courage

As the chief people officer of VICE Media Group, Daisy Auger-Dominguez has had years of experience with inclusivity. She has navigated difficult conversations, coached leaders at all levels of the organization, and has spent her career championing diversity, inclusion, equity, and belonging. As a leader who values transparency, Daisy shared the following in an article she wrote for the *Harvard Business Review*:

Last year, I sent a company-wide email denouncing anti-Semitism and Islamophobia, which drew attention from a group of Arab and Palestinian employees in our Middle East offices. A few days after receiving my note, they sent me a beautifully written, thoughtful response to offer an additional perspective on the content of my email. Specifically, they expressed disappointment about an article I linked to as a resource. They referred to a few points made in the article that may have unintentionally confused readers about anti-Semitism and Islamophobia during a particular time of crisis in Palestine. In my efforts to be inclusive, I had made some employees feel excluded.

There are two distinct ways to react when this happens. You can get defensive and explain the situation away. ("I didn't write the email without consulting others!" "You're missing the larger point and getting stuck in the details!") Or you can take full ownership of what happened, connect with those offended, and use it as a learning experience to try to do better. I bet you know which is the right answer.

I sent an email back admitting my mistake, which is that I had not thoroughly vetted my chosen resource with a broader subset of employees, including important regional voices, especially theirs. I apologized, took responsibility, and committed to do better next time.

We scheduled a meeting to connect and learn from this experience, and they helped me reflect on what I knew and didn't know about the complex and nuanced cultural matters in the Middle East. I was struck by their willingness to discuss these issues in a collaborative manner. In the end, it brought us closer and it remains one of the biggest lessons for me personally from last year.

I got called out, but they called me in.[16]

When she posted the HBR article on LinkedIn, Daisy added, "As leaders, we are responsible for understanding how our words land, naming what's confusing and hurtful, and exploring how to stay compassionate and awake to the needs of others. When we make a mistake, we must admit it, acknowledge the harm, apologize when we hurt someone, and commit to change our behavior."[17]

It takes courage to admit you were wrong. It takes **humility** to acknowledge you made a mistake. It takes **empathy** to hear how what you have done has harmed others and why. It takes **accountability** to stand up and take action to rectify the wrong. It takes **resiliency** to keep trying to get it right. It takes **transparency** to make this a learning opportunity for others. And it takes **inclusivity** to ensure your colleagues feel seen, connected, supported, and proud of the company and culture you are co-creating. In other words, it takes being committed to HEARTI to be a Modern Leader.

Be *that* leader.

The new way of work requires the next level of integrity, engagement, courage, and leadership. We will face embarrassment. We will make missteps. Those are inevitable moments in life. But we can pick ourselves up and do better next time.[18]

—Daisy Auger-Dominguez, chief people officer, VICE Media; and author of *The Inclusion Revolution: The Essential Guide to Dismantling Racial Equity in the Workplace*

5) Mixed Messages From Senior Leadership

Many senior leaders say they believe in DEIB and may even consider themselves champions; however, they often give employees mixed messages. For example, our Men@Work study revealed that male senior leaders are three times more likely than men at middle and junior levels to agree that "the focus on DEIB distracts employees from critical business issues." But these same leaders strongly agreed that DEIB delivers better outcomes for the business, makes their teams more innovative and successful, and even makes them better leaders. Huh?!

> *Too often corporate leaders are uncomfortable talking about DEI, fail to talk convincingly and authentically about the importance of DEI, or avoid uncomfortable conversations. It's time to center DEI as a strategic imperative.*
>
> **—Dr. David Smith, associate professor, Johns Hopkins Carey Business School; and coauthor of *Good Guys: How Men Can Be Better Allies for Women in the Workplace***

How do you solve these mixed messages? Take a cue from Hans Vestberg, chairman and CEO of Verizon Wireless, and make it transparent and accountable. "Because effective leadership is not based on what you say but what you do, we constantly track our effectiveness and have appointed an outside auditor to tell us objectively how we are doing and how we can improve," says Hans.[19] He believes, as we do, that your diversity and inclusion strategy must extend throughout the organization.

Janet M. Stovall, global head of DEI at the NeuroLeadership Institute and coauthor of *The Conscious Communicator: The Fine Art of Not Saying Stupid Sh*t*, agrees. She says, "When I started working in this space, DEI focused on interrupting bad behavior to minimize hostile workplaces, as well as to avoid lawsuits. Over time, it's evolved into a moral case—the right thing to do. Now, we've seen words like equity and belonging join the lexicon, and while these things are critical, what I see companies actually asking for is different. They want three things: proof that DEI investment efforts are providing positive returns; practicality in the form of actionable strategies; and progress, as evidenced by measurable improvement in key performance indicators."[20]

The only way to achieve both proof and practicality, which then enables progress, is by viewing DEIB as a business asset with a triple bottom-line business value that solves the big problems facing our company and our world. When diversity is prioritized organizationally, it can be leveraged through inclusive habits and then sustained by systems of equity.

One critical solution for the internal and external forces that can hold leaders back from inclusion is lack of access to Modern Leadership training and development programs. After completing one of PrismWork's inclusive leadership learning labs, a Fortune 500 global leader told us, "Thanks to this program, I have the confidence and belief I can take things on. I am thinking much broader about equity at my company—not just the department I work in, but the company overall and how I can be a facilitator of change more globally."

Spoken like a Modern Leader committed to triple bottom-line impact.

Disrupting the Status Quo

When it comes to DEIB, Christina Blacken, founder of The New Quo, a leadership development and inclusion consultancy, believes using our power with intention to disrupt the status quo is the only way to drive real change. Christina grew up in Utah, one of the only Black kids in her almost exclusively Mormon community. This meant, as she says, "Racially, religiously, and politically, I was on the outskirts of the majority."[21] Being an outsider enabled Christina to see things through a different but multifaceted lens.

She recognizes how and why Traditional Leadership and shareholder capitalism (old power) has been holding back so many of us, especially previously underrepresented talent. As Christina explains it, "Conventional business models are designed by default to be inequitable. The core value of this conventional model is a hoarding and imbalance of resources which provides capital for the owners and executives, while extracting as much value as possible from the consumers and employees."

"As a result," says Christina, "leaders hire for diversity with the belief that this is going to solve issues of inequality, without thinking about why and how the business models we operate from create inequality itself, regardless of who is leading them. It's an important step to have a better balance of demographics and identities at the top, middle, and bottom of the pyramid of an organization—yet if that pyramid is flawed itself, with hoarding and power imbalances as its continued drivers, it's only a power swap that's occurring, not a power restructuring that leads to real, equitable change."

So what exactly is a power restructuring? Well, it depends. For some it is a complete overhaul of capitalism, but that's not where we stand. For us, it's about moving from shareholder capitalism to stakeholder capitalism. It's about recognizing that new power must be focused on positive change. It's about providing the opportunity for leaders at all levels and from all backgrounds to step into power and demonstrate their power in a more just and inclusive way.

Here's the deal: If you aren't truly, in your heart, committed to DEIB, you're thinking like a Traditional Leader and are not only outdated but at risk of being replaced by a Modern Leader with a "we" mindset. When it comes down to it, the leaders who don't really either understand or believe that DEIB is directly linked to triple bottom-line impact are the leaders who are going to lose in the years to come. Don't be one of the losers.

Until we have true accountability that requires leaders to be inclusive, DE&I is a choice for those who are part of the majority. But by choosing to not engage, you lose the opportunity to attract and retain the top talent which hurts your company and you.

—Lybra Clemons, Chief Diversity Officer, Twilio

Reframe

Inclusivity Is a Power Skill

- Attracts and retains diverse talent for a sustainable talent pipeline;
- Expands your options for succession planning;
- Provides a more complete picture of challenges and opportunities;
- Supports more informed decision-making;
- Drives increased innovation;
- Enhances trust;
- Promotes curiosity, courage, and a growth mindset;
- Delivers better performance by leveraging a variety of perspectives and experiences;
- Is the foundation for delivering on the triple bottom line.

Evolving Your Leadership

Ten Questions to Increase Your Inclusivity

Self:

1) How can I ensure my behaviors and actions are aligned with my why?

2) What actions can I take to disrupt biases in myself and others?

3) How can I cultivate supportive, collaborative, reciprocal relationships with diverse talent?

4) What can I do to get more informed about systems of oppression?

5) What more do I need to learn and do to increase my inclusive leadership competencies?

Systems:

6) How do I collaborate with others to create policies and procedures that work for everyone within my company?

7) How do I make sure these initiatives are measured and tracked to ensure our company and its leaders are accountable?

8) How do I establish and support systems that hold others accountable for creating inclusive cultures?

(*continued*)

Society:

9) How do I courageously and publicly advocate for all by championing diversity in my industry and in society at large?

10) How can I take action to ensure sustainable outcomes for all stakeholders within my organization and beyond?

9

Live Your Impact

HERE we are, the last "class," and arguably the most important. You've made it this far because you're driven by a purpose far greater than yourself and have been looking for the insights, framework, and tools to be the leader we all need you to be. You know you have power and want to use your power with intention to drive long-term, sustainable success for yourself, your company, and the world we all live in.

Thank you. No, seriously, thank you.

In a world so confused and chaotic, it is a relief to know there are leaders out there committed to doing the hard work to create a better world for the generations to come. We love that about you.

But aspiration alone is not enough to be a Modern Leader who drives triple bottom-line impact.

It seems obvious, but so often we forget this simple truth: companies are made up by a collection of people who agree to commit their skills and abilities to an agreed-upon goal. It's the people who work for the companies that are making the impact. They are the ones whose wisdom, talent, insights, and actions are driving the change. This means the responsibility to make impact is not on the company per se, but on the leaders who work at those companies. And, as we have explained, every single person at every level of the organization can and must see themselves as the leaders they are, so this means the responsibility is on you. All of which is to say, *your* leadership purpose is essential for triple bottom-line impact.

Your Leadership Purpose

It might be hard to believe, but the notion of "leadership purpose" is relatively new. Discussions around the concept really took off in the rubble of the 2008 financial crisis. After losing their jobs, their retirement savings, and, for far too many, their homes, people started asking themselves, "Why the heck am I working this hard?" *and* "Who really benefits when I do?"

Sound familiar? They're the same questions so many have asked in the rubble of Covid. The same questions that drove the Great Resignation, Quiet Quitting, and the ones that have kept employees disengaged for decades. Work *has to mean more than a paycheck* for ourselves and a windfall for investors. Full stop.

Enter your leadership purpose. No question that if you have clarity on your purpose and can link it to your daily economic activity, the work in general, and hard work in particular, makes sense. A study by McKinsey revealed nearly 70% of professionals consider work a key component of defining their purpose. The study also showed that when employees at any level say that their purpose is aligned with their work, the positive outcomes in both their work *and* personal lives are anywhere from two to five times higher than those reported by their peers who aren't aligned.[1] Why? Because purpose-fueled work moves people off the hamster wheel of striving on to a journey that often results in thriving.

The data also confirms having purpose is good for our overall well-being. Dr. Dhruv Khullar, a physician and assistant professor of health policy and economics at Weill Cornell Medical College, says, "Having purpose is linked to a number of positive health outcomes, including better sleep, fewer strokes and heart attacks, and a lower risk of dementia, disability and premature death. Those with a strong sense of purpose are more likely to embrace preventive health services, like mammograms, colonoscopies and flu shots."[2] One study followed more than 6,000 individuals over 14 years and found that those with greater purpose were 15 percent less likely to die than those who were aimless and that having clarity on one's purpose was protective across the life span—for people in their 20s as well as those in their 70s.[3]

So having a purpose can help us be healthier. Great! But, can it also help our careers? "Yes!" says leadership expert Nick Craig. In 2014, he and his colleague Scott Snook wrote a seminal article for the *Harvard Business Review* where they explained,

> Your leadership purpose is who you are and what makes you distinctive. Whether you're an entrepreneur at a start-up or the CEO of a *Fortune* 500 company, a call center rep or a software developer, your purpose is your brand, what you're driven to achieve, the magic that makes you tick. It's not *what* you do—it's *why*—the strengths and passions you bring to the table no matter where you're seated.[4]

When we spoke to Nick in 2023, he told us that in his experience those leaders who were able to get very clear on their purpose ended up with more rewarding, more impactful, and more successful careers. "Purpose allows a leader to powerfully access both head and heart. When we speak from this place in ourselves, it changes not just the leader but everyone else around them. This level of congruency and passion is contagious. In this way, leaders with purpose are growing followers with a deeper sense of mission, which also generates significantly better business outcomes."

He's right. You may remember in Chapter 2, "Intentional Power," we shared that when the CEO emphasized stakeholder values, followers were more likely to view them as visionary leaders. And when employees saw their leaders as visionary, they expended more effort, and their companies saw increased financial performance. Meanwhile, Gallup confirms that purpose is one of the most important drivers of employee engagement and is the greatest overall predictor of talent retention and optimization.[5] In other words, aligning work with purpose is good for employees and good for the bottom line.

But purpose can be confusing, and for many of us, overwhelming. As one of our coaching clients shared, "Find my purpose? Ha! I'm working so hard, I just want to get through the day."

Nick Craig says this is a flawed approach. He believes the most important developmental task of a leader is to articulate your purpose *and then have the courage to live it*. And it doesn't have to be some earth-shattering life-changing experience. For the vast majority of leaders Nick has worked with finding their purpose "wasn't about quitting their job and going to work for Save the Children, or leaving their spouse, or telling their boss to stuff it; it was about realizing that purpose is present in every moment, and we can choose to operate from it or not."[6] In other words, whether you know it or not, you are already living your purpose.

> *Purpose is an essential element of you. It is the reason you are on the planet at this particular time in history. Your very existence is wrapped up in the things you are here to fulfill. Whatever you choose for a career path, remember, the struggles along the way are only meant to shape you for your purpose.*
>
> **—Dr. Chadwick Boseman, actor and humanitarian, Howard University Commencement Address 2018**[7]

Earlier in her career, Shirley Turner, who is now executive director, Reach Northwest, and one of our executive coaching clients, was a vice president at a technology company. She crafted a mantra she called "ELM"—essential, lead, move. For

Shirley, focusing on the Essential work by setting clear priorities, Leading the disparate personalities on her team through inspiration, and Moving decisively and quickly, both in making work decisions and in getting physical activity for her health, was the inspiration she needed to stay purpose-aligned. Shirley often symbolized her "ELM" mantra by doodling a small image of a leaf on her daily schedule or in the corner of note pages. An elm leaf necklace had her, as she calls it, "clutching her ELM"—rather than "clutching her pearls"—to ground herself during surprising moments. Those prompts helped her align everyday actions with her purpose. In time, the clarity ELM brought Shirley helped her move from corporate technology senior management to nonprofit leadership. The stage and audience changed, but the mantra remained the same.

Leader Tool Kit

How to Find Your Purpose by Recognizing Your Impact

Understanding your leadership purpose requires you to look back at the patterns of your life, aligning those patterns with what you value, using that to define your overall purpose. Then, consider how you can bring that to your work so you can make an impact.

How do you do that? Start by taking some time to reflect on your values and the leader you aspire to be. What matters most to you? If you struggle with this exercise, you might begin with an online assessment, like the Center for Greater Good, UC Berkeley's Purpose Quiz,[8] Brene Brown's *Dare to Lead* values exercise or her podcast *Unlocking Us*

(*continued*)

episode focused on "Living Into Our Values" (downloadable. pdf).[9]

1) What three accomplishments have others told you positively impacted them?

2) What stakeholders benefited from these three accomplishments?

3) In the future, who would you like to benefit from your efforts?

4) What three things will they be able to do in the future that they aren't able to do today because of your impact?

Now, visualize a future celebration and map your path to impact.

You're being honored for the impact of your efforts at an awards ceremony 10 or 20 years in the future. What are the accomplishments you're being congratulated for? Who benefited from your work? What about your achievement makes you most proud?

Now, as that future-self, write a short letter, giving your current-self advice on the path ahead. What values did you live to deliver this impact? What HEARTI skills did you use? What were key turning points or choices that provided valuable experiences on your road to success? What obstacles did you overcome? What types of people or communities were essential to helping you grow and evolve so you could deliver the impact? Focusing on your ideal self and environment can increase your optimism, which is tied to purpose.

It takes intentional action built on having clarity on your purpose to drive triple bottom-line impact. So do the work, get clear on your purpose, and the sooner, the better. Because once you get that clarity, the real work begins.

The HOW of Driving Triple Bottom-Line Impact

Getting clear on your purpose is essential to being a Modern Leader. But to deliver triple bottom-line impact, purpose is not enough. Purpose is personal. It is focused on "me"—in other words, inwardly focused. Impact is about what you do for others. It is outwardly focused. Modern Leaders know that purpose is the fuel that inspires them to take actions that have impact far beyond themselves.

Modern Leaders are change makers committed to action.

How do they take action to make an impact? It's about moving between three key levels of impact: *self, systems,* and *society.* The three levels of impact is rooted in your why (i.e. your purpose) and then radiates out from your why to how you show up in your relationships (*self*), how you drive change within your company (*systems*), and what you do for the benefit of *society* overall.

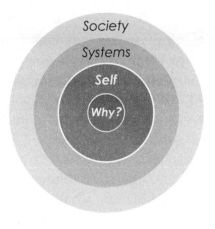

You may have noticed as you've read through *Intentional Power* we have been indirectly and even overtly (Remember: 300% accountability) weaving in three levels of impact as examples of how Modern Leaders evolve themselves to become the agents of change we all need. We showed how they move from *Self* (as Clark Murphy did when he realized he wanted to champion sustainability), to *Systems* (as Indra Nooyi did when she worked to pivot PepsiCo from single bottom line to triple bottom line), to *Society* (as Yvon Chouinard did when he pushed his company to positively impact the planet).

Changing YourSELF

Gray Clark of Dell Technologies is a Modern Leader who uses HEARTI as a framework for himself and his team. He first took our class in the fall of 2021. The insights and structure enabled him to be more authentic as a leader, sharing more of himself, which encouraged others to do so as well. In 2023, Gray came back as a guest executive to talk about how he has evolved his impact for his team of 125 system engineers.

Gray shared, "I'm an engineer and lead a presales team for a big tech company, but I'm also a mindfulness practitioner. For a long time, I kept that part of myself hidden from work. Frankly, I worried they'd think I was some kind of weirdo. But as the intensity and stress of Covid weighed down on us, I decided to launch an online morning mindfulness meditation practice for anyone in the company who wanted to attend." Each week, Gray would bring his insights and experience with mindfulness to anyone at Dell who wanted to show up. And many, many did. The class was such a success that it is now available globally through Dell's partnership with Virgin Pulse.

Moving from purpose to impact doesn't have to be about moving mountains. As Gray says, "Purpose is not so much 'finding' it as it is living it. Often, we think of purpose as some noble event that it is something we strive to attain. We think that 'someday' we will live our purpose when we make a certain amount of money or have a certain title. Some of the greatest servant leaders in history did not have a title or a big salary—yet we see in them their purpose as the impact of their actions lives on in their legacy."

As for Gray's career? It's on fire! He has been promoted and is now serving on numerous internal leadership teams helping to foster a more inclusive, welcoming culture at Dell. By living his why, Gray was able to share his passion for mindfulness to support his colleagues and gain in the process as well. Gray told our class, "There are many days after a meditation class when I literally call or text my manager and say, 'I can't believe you paid me for what I got to do today.'"

Now that is HEARTI in action.

Changing Your Company's SYSTEMS

When Mary Beth Laughton was appointed as CEO of Athleta in 2019, she came with a mission: empower women. In a 2022 op-ed for CNN, Mary Beth wrote, "When I started my career in the late 1990s, only six women had ever broken the proverbial glass ceiling to become CEOs of Fortune 500 companies. . . . Last year, the number of women running businesses on the Fortune 500 hit a record of 41. And while I'm proud to be one of the women who lead billion-dollar brands, there still aren't enough of us. Businesses can play a key role in supporting women, and some have already taken action to create a culture and business that prioritizes them. Now, it's time for all companies to work on leveraging these opportunities (and finding new ones) to be a catalyst for change."[10]

Athleta had already committed to pay equity for women before she arrived, but Mary Beth quickly expanded the company's focus on pay fairness to include an analysis of racial disparities. Today, with a continued commitment to full transparency, Athleta's website states, "Starting in 2020, we now have an external firm assess our pay data by race for US employees, with the objective of continuing to ensure pay equity for all employees. This independent review concluded by finding no meaningful pay disparity by gender or race."[11]

Mary Beth didn't stop there. To be more inclusive with their product offerings, she expanded the size offerings to run from XXS to 3X, rolled out mannequins in all shapes and sizes, and trained its 5,500 store associates in inclusive clothing options. She also looked outside the company to determine how Athleta could have a greater impact. In 2021, Athleta partnered with Allyson Felix, Simone Biles, and Alicia Keys to not only collaborate on traditional product offerings but also advise on and amplify initiatives like the Power of She Fund to provide grants aimed at recognizing female empowerment. In partnership with Allyson, Simone, and Alicia, the Fund has collectively awarded more than $1.4 million to more than 50 organizations to date, positively impacting more than 10,000 women and girls.[12]

Mary Beth concluded her 2022 op-ed by writing, "Investing in women is an investment for all, because when a woman is empowered, she lifts up other women, their families and their communities to build a more equitable and just world."

Yep.

You Need to Know

B Certified = The Best Way to Measure Triple Bottom-Line Impact

At the start of this book, we identified that one of the biggest challenges leaders are facing is how to navigate the move from shareholder to stakeholder capitalism. Yes, a mindset shift is essential, but how does a leader measure success? We mentioned the rise—and current pushback—of ESG as a measurement model. But there is a much better alternative: B Certification.

The B Corp Certification was established in 2007 by B Lab Global, a nonprofit dedicated to transforming the global economy to benefit all people, communities, and the planet. Being B Corp certified means that a business meets high standards of verified performance, accountability, and transparency on factors from employee benefits and charitable giving to supply chain practices and input materials.[13]

Certified Benefit Corporations (B Corps) are the definition of companies dedicated to triple bottom-line outcomes. Athleta is a great example of a B Certified Company.

Changing SOCIETY

Maria Colacurcio is passionate about economic equality and believes "Every. Single. Person." should be paid fairly and equitably. She also believes strongly that in today's working environment, pay equity is foundational to a company's success. According to Maria, "The way that we treat our people—with fairness, with respect, and with equitable programs and policies is not a nice to have, it's paramount to whether our companies succeed or fail."

To make her passion and purpose a reality, she joined Syndio as CEO in 2018—a technology start-up that uses a SaaS solution to drive equity in the workplace. Syndio's software enables companies to ensure they are delivering pay equity to their employees. In partnership with Fair Pay Workplace, Syndio also provides third-party validation for companies that want to ensure their employees know they are paid fairly.

When Maria joined the company there were nine employees and, as she says, "a really good idea." Today, Syndio serves 268 companies such as Nordstrom, General Mills, and Volvo. In doing so, it has helped put $1.9 million back into the pockets of previously inequitably paid employees. Not only have employees benefited, but Syndio has also helped companies reduce the amount of pay remediation by 17%—a win for all.

Being a Modern Leader committed to making triple bottom-line impact isn't easy. "It's hard as hell to run a B2B tech start-up," says Maria, "but the energy I get from the impact I know our company is making gives me the fuel I need to keep going when the days are hard."

> *The purpose of leadership is not to make the present bearable. The purpose of leadership is to make the future possible.*
> **—Joan D. Chittiser, Benedictine Sister of Erie**

Leader Tool Kit

How Modern Leaders Use Their Power with Intention for the Benefit of All Stakeholders

Self

- Know their WHY;
- Take a stand on issues that align with their leadership purpose;
- Engage and lift employees to optimize their impact.

Systems

- Drive company programs and policies that promote fairness and equity;

- Enroll others in a collective mission to benefit people, planet, and profits;
- Create and deliver recognition that celebrates both the *what* and the *how.*

Society

- Publicly declare their commitment to triple bottom-line impact;
- Take stands on the hard issues facing stakeholders;
- Use their power and privilege to benefit all stakeholders.

These leaders model the *how* of driving triple bottom-line impact. Not every Modern Leader is going to be operating at every level of impact at all times. We invite you to consider what level of impact you are tackling as you evolve your Modern Leadership.

Your Intentional Power

Which brings us full circle back to your intentional power. We started this book by declaring the Modern Leader's purpose and responsibility. As a Modern Leader, it is incumbent upon you to use your power for the benefit of more than your career and more than your company's bottom line. With HEARTI as your fuel, we want you to achieve your wildest dreams professionally, and we urge you to make sure that as you are achieving those dreams, you are using your power with purpose and intention.

Thus, the Modern Leader's credo becomes the HEARTI leader's credo.

The HEARTI Leader's Goal

Inspire free people, cultures, and societies to move courageously toward mutually beneficial positions where all can thrive.

The HEARTI Leader's Responsibility

Create and maintain environments that encourage confidence, creativity, and constructive change where all stakeholders prosper.

Phew. We're here. The last paragraph in the last chapter of this book and, we hope, the start of the next phase of your journey as a HEARTI leader committed to making a positive impact for generations to come. We've given you tools, shared stories, profiled leaders, and grounded it all in research and data for proof against any lingering doubts, all with the goal of arming you for the urgent work of leading today for the tomorrows to come. We invite you to remember, everything you fight for is not for yourself; it is for those who come after you. Our student Abel said it best when he quoted Jewish religious sage and scholar Rabbi Hillel, "If I am not for myself, then who will be for me? And if I am only for myself, then what am I? And if not now, when?"

The Time Is Now. Lead On!

Acknowledgments

THIS book was the outgrowth of our classes at Stanford University's Continuing Studies program, corporate workshops, and speaking engagements delivered around the world. To our students and clients, thanks for challenging us to improve our thinking, refine the HEARTI model, and clarify our explanations. To all our guest executive speakers, thank you for being vulnerable and transparent in sharing the peaks and valleys of your careers. Whether or not your story was included in this book, know that your impact on hundreds of leaders is rippling through many industries.

This project wouldn't have come to fruition without the faith and full support of our team at Wiley. Thanks, Brian Neill, for believing in us, Julie Kerr, for holding us accountable, and Deborah Schindlar, for overseeing the effort. A special shout out to Wiley sales for their feedback and partnership in focusing the impact of this book.

To our PrismWork collaborators and advisors, thanks for keeping it real! This book was years in the making, and you lived through each iteration. We can't thank you enough for providing practical and moral support as we failed forward. And to our clients, thank you for your collaboration. It has been an honor to join you on your leadership journeys to fostering companies that deliver the triple bottom line.

Finally, it is with deepest gratitude that we would like to acknowledge our families for giving us the time "away" to bring this book to fruition. Coordinating across time zones and three family systems required flexibility, patience, and a whole lotta love. We wrote this book because we want the world to be a better place for you.

The seed you plant in love, no matter how small, will grow into a mighty tree of refuge. We all want a future for ourselves, and we must now care enough to create, nurture, and secure a future for our children.

—**Afeni Shakur**

Notes

Chapter 1

1) Creditors Adjustment Bureau. (2022). "Building a multi-generational workforce" (20 July). https://cabcollects.com/building-a-multigenerational-workforce/#:~:text=In%20 2025%2C%20baby%20boomers%20will,of%20the%20 U.S.%20labor%20force.

2) Company IQ Insights. (2022). "Is there an optimal level of CEO experience to run America's largest companies?" MyLogiq (9 March). https://www.mylogiq.com/archives/ insight/is-there-an-optimal-level-of-ceo-experience-to-run-americas-largest-companies#:~:text=81%25%20of% 20S%26P%20500%20CEOs,500%20CEO%20tenure%20 is%207.

3) Miller, K., and Riley, J. (2022). "Changed landscape, unchanged norms: Work-family conflict and the persistence of the academic mother ideal." *Innovative Higher Education* 47(2). http://doi.org/10.1007/s10755-021-09586-2.

4) Microsoft. (2021). 2021 Work Trend Index: Annual Report. https://www.microsoft.com/en-us/worklab/work-trend-index/hybrid-work.

5) Aziz, A. (2020). "Global study reveals consumers are four to six times more likely to purchase, protect and champion purpose-driven companies." *Forbes* (17 June). https://www.forbes.com/sites/afdhelaziz/2020/06/17/global-study-reveals-consumers-are-four-to-six-times-more-likely-to-purchase-protect-and-champion-purpose-driven-companies/?sh=2dec57b1435f.

6) Edelman. (2023). "2023 Edelman trust barometer: Navigating a polarized world." https://www.edelman.com/trust/2023/trust-barometer.

7) Wells, H. (2021). "The purpose of a corporation: A brief history." The Temple 10-Q. https://www2.law.temple.edu/10q/purpose-corporation-brief-history/.

8) Friedman, M. (1970). "A Friedman doctrine—the social responsibility of business is to increase its profits." *The New York Times* (13 September), section SM, p. 17. https://www.nytimes.com/1970/09/13/archives/a-friedman-doctrine-the-social-responsibility-of-business-is-to.html.

9) Daly, L. (2023). "How many Americans own stock? About 150 million—but the wealthiest 1% own more than half." The Motley Fool (19 January). https://www.fool.com/research/how-many-americans-own-stock/.

10) The World Bank. (2023). "Inequality and shared prosperity." https://www.worldbank.org/en/topic/isp.

11) Cohen, B. (2006). *Values-Driven Business: How to Change the World, Make Money, and Have Fun.* Oakland, CA: Berrett-Koehler Publishers.

12) Ulukaya, H. (2019). "The anti-CEO playbook." TED. https://www.ted.com/talks/hamdi_ulukaya_the_anti_ceo_playbook?language=en.

13) Fink, L. (2022). "The power of capitalism." BlackRock. https://www.blackrock.com/corporate/investor-relations/larry-fink-ceo-letter.

14) Business Roundtable. (2019). "Business Roundtable redefines the purpose of a corporation to promote 'an economy that serves all Americans.'" Business Roundtable (19 August). https://www.businessroundtable.org/business-roundtable-redefines-the-purpose-of-a-corporation-to-promote-an-economy-that-serves-all-americans.

15) Ibid.

16) Stevens, P. (2020). "Stakeholder capitalism has reached a 'tipping point,' says Salesforce CEO Benioff." CNBC (21 January). https://www.cnbc.com/2020/01/21/stakeholder-capitalism-has-reached-a-tipping-point-says-salesforce-ceo-benioff.html.

17) Fink, L. (2022). "The power of capitalism." BlackRock.

18) Kadri, I. (2023). Twitter post (22 March). https://twitter.com/Kadriilham/status/1638602035133071361.

19) Solvay. (2022). "Solvay One Planet Progress." https://www.solvay.com/en/investors/toward-sustainable-investing-esg-information/solvay-one-planet-progress.

20) Randall, S. (2020). "Companies that prioritize sustainability outperform for investors." Wealth Professional Canada (21 January). https://www.wealthprofessional.ca/news/industry-news/companies-that-prioritize-sustainability-outperform-for-investors/325241.

21) Service Now. https://www.servicenow.com/company/global-impact.html.

22) Nasdaq. (2021). "What is ESG investing and why is it worth trillions?" Nasdaq (15 July). https://www.nasdaq.com/articles/what-is-esg-investing-and-why-is-it-worth-trillions-2021-07-15.

23) McKinsey & Company. (2020). "Why ESG is here to stay." Podcast(26 May). https://www.mckinsey.com/capabilities/strategy-and-corporate-finance/our-insights/why-esg-is-here-to-stay.

24) United Nations. "Transforming our world: The 2030 agenda for sustainable development." https://sustainabledevelopment.un.org/content/documents/21252030%20Agenda%20for%20Sustainable%20Development%20web.pdf.

25) Harper, E. (2022). *Move to the Edge, Declare it Center*. Hoboken, NJ: Wiley, p. 3.

Chapter 2

1) Wallace, D.F. (2005). "This is water." Commencement address to Kenyon College. https://fs.blog/david-foster-wallace-this-is-water/.

2) de Luque, M.S., Washburn, N.T., Waldman, D.A., and House, R.J. (2008). "Unrequited profit: How stakeholder and economic values relate to subordinates' perceptions of leadership and firm performance." *Administrative Science Quarterly* 53(4): 626–654. https://doi.org/10.2189/asqu.53.4.626.

3) Department of the Army. (2019). "Army leadership and the profession (ADP 6-22)." Army Doctrine Publication (July). https://irp.fas.org/doddir/army/adp6_22.pdf.

4) Benioff, Marc. (2019, October 15). *Trailblazer: The Power of Business as the Greatest Platform for Change*, Currency/Crown Publishing.

5) Beer. J. (2018). "Exclusive: 'Patagonia is in the business to save our home planet.'" *Fast Company* (13 December). https://www.fastcompany.com/90280950/exclusive-patagonia-is-in-business-to-save-our-home-planet.

6) Chouinard, Y. "Earth is now our only shareholder." Patagonia. https://www.patagonia.com/ownership/.

7) Ibid.

8) People Powered Innovation Collaborative (PPIC). (2016). "Performance with a purpose at PepsiCo." PepsiCo (21 September). https://ppicollaborative.org/NuWorld/wp-ontent/uploads/PepsiCo-21-09-16.pdf.

9) Tom (2017). "Performance with purpose: PepsiCo's sustainability mission." MBA Student Perspectives, Harvard University. https://d3.harvard.edu/platform-rctom/submis sion/performance-with-purpose-pepsicos-sustainability-mission/.

10) Nooyi, I. (2016). "10 years ago, I said PepsiCo had to be about more than making money. Here's what's in store for the next 10." LinkedIn (17 October). https://www.linkedin.com/pulse/10-years-ago-i-said-pepsico-had-more-than-making-money-indra-nooyi/.

11) Murphy, C. (2022). *Sustainable Leadership: Lessons of Vision, Courage, and Grit From the CEOs Who Dared to Build a Better World.* Hoboken, NJ: Wiley, p. 8.

12) Purushathoman, D. (2022). *The First, The Few, the Only: How Women of Color Can Redefine Power in Corporate America.* New York: Harper Business, p. 190.

13) Gwin, B.W., Hanson, J.C., Sanderes, J.S., Taylor, L.A. (2023). "Board monitor US 2023." Heidrick & Struggles. https://www.heidrick.com/en/insights/boards-governance/board-monitor-us-2023.

14) Purushathoman, D. (2022). *The First, The Few, the Only: How Women of Color Can Redefine Power in Corporate America,* p. 190.

15) Bersin, J. (2020). "Let's stop talking about soft skills: They're power skills. JoshBersin.com" (16 November). https://joshbersin.com/2019/10/lets-stop-talking-about-soft-skills-theyre-power-skills/.

16) Ibid.

17) Udemy Business. (2022). "2022 Workplace learning trends report." https://business.udemy.com/2022-workplace-lear ning-trends-report/?utm_source=organic-search&utm_ medium=google.

Chapter 3

1) Power Lunch. (2019). "Why this exec tells employees to 'stop apologizing for having lives.'" CNBC (13 June). https://www .cnbc.com/video/2019/06/13/why-this-exec-tells-employees-to-stop-apologizing-for-having-lives.html.

2) Mandela, Nelson. *Long Walk to Freedom*, Little Brown & Co, 1994.

3) Kapsos, S. (2021). "Why would labour productivity surge during a pandemic?" ILOSTAT (14 December). https:// ilostat.ilo.org/why-would-labour-productivity-surge-during-a-pandemic/.

4) Marshall, E.D. (2021). "Working from home 'doesn't work for those who don't want to hustle'": JPMorgan CEO. Reuters (4 May). https://www.reuters.com/article/us-jp-morgan-ceo/working-from-home-doesnt-work-for-those-who-want-to-hustle-jpmorgan-ceo-idUSKBN2CL1HQ.

5) Department of the Army. (2019). "Army leadership and the profession (ADP 6-22)." Army Doctrine Publication (July). https://irp.fas.org/doddir/army/adp6_22.pdf.

6) Goodwin, D.K. (2005). *Team of Rivals*. New York: Simon & Schuster.

7) Prime, Jeanine, and Salib, Elizabeth R. (2014). "Inclusive Leadership: The View from Six Countries." Catalyst (May 7). https://www.catalyst.org/research/inclusive-leadership-the-view-from-six-countries/.

8) Ou, A.Y., Walkman, D.A., and Peterson, S.J. (2015). "Do humble CEOs matter? An examination of CEO humility and firm outcomes." *Journal of Management* 44(3): 1147–1173. https://doi.org/10.1177/0149206315604187.

9) PercentSolution. (2014, November 6). The 3% Conference John Gerzema keynote: *64,000 People Can't Be Wrong.* [Video]. YouTube. https://www.youtube.com/watch?v=8Wy m3eKHFIg

10) Chamorro-Premuzic, Thomas. (2019, March 12). *Why Do So Many Incompetent Men Become Leaders?* Harvard Business Review Press.

11) Smith, David G., and Johnson, W. Brad. (2020). *Good Guys: How Men Can Be Better Allies for Women in the Workplace.* Boston: Harvard Business Review Press, p. 63.

12) Chesky, B., and Lin, A. (2014). "Lecture 10—Culture." Y Combinator: The Vault. YouTube video. https://www.youtube .com/watch?v=RfWgVWGEuGE.

13) Ballard, J. (2021). "Most 'complete extroverts' say their partners are extroverts too; introverts are more split." YouGov (16 July). https://today.yougov.com/topics/ society/articles-reports/2021/07/16/extroverts-introverts-dating-poll-data.

14) Susan Cain, 2012 TED Talk, "The Power of Introverts." https://www.ted.com/talks/susan_cain_the_power_of_ introverts?language=en.

15) PowHer Redefined, www.powherredefined.com.

16) "The high cost of a toxic workplace culture." (2020). SHRM. https://pmq.shrm.org/wp-content/uploads/2020/07/ SHRM-Culture-Report_2019-1.pdf.

17) Sull, D., Sull, C., and Zweig, B. (2022). "Toxic culture is driving the great resignation." *MIT Sloan Management Review* (11 January). https://sloanreview.mit.edu/article/ toxic-culture-is-driving-the-great-resignation/.

18) Department of the Army. (2019). "Army leadership and the profession (ADP 6-22)." Army Doctrine Publication (July). https://irp.fas.org/doddir/army/adp6_22.pdf.

19) Eurich, Tasha. (October 19, 2018). *Working With People Who Aren't Self-Aware.* Harvard Business Review. https://hbr .org/2018/10/working-with-people-who-arent-self-aware.

Chapter 4

1) Elias, J. (2022). "Google CEO tells employees productivity and focus must improve, launches 'Simplicity Sprint' to gather employee feedback on efficiency." CNBC (1 August). https://www.cnbc.com/2022/07/31/google-ceo-to-employees-productivity-and-focus-must-improve.html.

2) Sinek, Simon. (2018, June 20). Facebook. https://www.facebook.com/simonsinek/posts/10156462608691499/

3) Morning Future. (2018, June 18). "Satya Nadella: when empathy is good for business." https://www.morningfuture.com/en/2018/06/18/microsoft-satya-nadella-empathy-business-management/.

4) Stein, D., Hobson, N., Jachimowicz, J.M., and Whillans, A. (2021). "How companies can improve employee engagement right now." *Harvard Business Review* (13 October). https://hbr.org/2021/10/how-companies-can-improve-employee-engagement-right-now.

5) Van Brommel, T. (2021). "The power of empathy in times of crisis and beyond." Catalyst. https://www.catalyst.org/reports/empathy-work-strategy-crisis.

6) Zenger, J. and Folkman, J. (2022). "Quiet quitting is about bad bosses, not bad employees." *Harvard Business Review* (31 August). https://hbr.org/2022/08/quiet-quitting-is-about-bad-bosses-not-bad-employees.

7) Van Brommel, T. (2021). "The power of empathy in times of crisis and beyond." Catalyst. https://www.catalyst.org/reports/empathy-work-strategy-crisis.

8) Barsh, J., Capozzi, M.M., and Davidson, J. (2008). "Leadership and innovation." *McKinsey Quarterly* (1 January). https://www.mckinsey.com/capabilities/strategy-and-corporate-finance/our-insights/leadership-and-innovation.

9) Business Solver. (2021). "State of workplace empathy." https://www.businesssolver.com/workplace-empathy/.

10) Van Brommel, T. (2021). "The power of empathy in times of crisis and beyond." Catalyst. https://www.catalyst.org/reports/empathy-work-strategy-crisis.

11) Stewart, W.F., Ricci, J.A., Chee, E., Hahn, S.R., and Morganstein, D. (2003). "Cost of Lost Productive Work Time among US Workers with Depression." *JAMA*. (June 18) 289(23): 3135–3144. https://doi:10.1001/jama.289.23.3135.

12) Business Solver. (2021). "Declining mental health requires employer empathy." https://resources.businessolver.com/declining-mental-health-requires-employer-empathy/declining-mental-health-WP.

13) Wilkinson, H., Whittington, R., Perry, L., and Eames, C. (2017). "Examining the relationship between burnout and empathy in healthcare professionals: A systematic review." *Burnout Research* 6: 18–29. http://doi:10.1016/j.burn.2017.06.003.

14) Thomson, S. (2016, November 18). "10 companies that are great at empathy." World Economic Forum. https://www.weforum.org/agenda/2016/11/empathy-index-business/.

15) Denning, S. (2021, July 18). "How empathy helped generate a $2 trillion company." *Forbes*. https://www.forbes.com/sites/stevedenning/2021/07/18/how-empathy-helped-generate-a-two-trillion-dollar-company/.

16) Nadella, S. (2017). *Hit Refresh: The Quest to Rediscover Microsoft's Soul and Imagine a Better Future for Everyone*. New York: HarperCollins.

17) Du, J., Huang, S., Lu, Q., Ma, L., Lai, K., and Li, K. (2022). "Influence of empathy and professional values on ethical decision-making of emergency nurses: A cross sectional study." *International Emergency Nursing* 63:101186. https://doi.org/10.1016/j.ienj.2022.101186.

18) Cartabuke, M., Westerman, J.W., Bergman, J.Z., et al. (2019). "Empathy as an antecedent of social justice attitudes and perceptions." *Journal of Business Ethics* 157: 605–615. https://doi.org/10.1007/s10551-017-3677-1.

19) Cameron, C.D., Conway, P., and Scheffer, J.A. (2022). "Empathy regulation, prosociality, and moral judgment." *Current Opinion in Psychology* 44: 188–195. https://doi.org/10.1016/j.copsyc.2021.09.011.

20) Allen, S. (2017, April 26). "Can empathy protect you from burnout?" *Great Good Magazine.* https://greatergood.berkeley.edu/article/item/can_empathy_protect_you_from_burnout.

21) Yue, Z., Qin, Y., Li, Y. et al. (2022). "Empathy and burnout in medical staff: Mediating role of job satisfaction and job commitment." *BMC Public Health* 22: 1033. https://doi.org/10.1186/s12889-022-13405-4.

22) Brown, Brene, (2013, December 10). "Brene Brown on Empathy" RSA.org, YouTube video 0:2:53. https://youtu.be/1Evwgu369Jw.

23) Gentry, W.A., Weber, T.J., and Sadri, G. (2016). "Empathy in the workplace: A tool for effective leadership." Center for Creative Leadership. https://cclinnovation.org/wp-content/uploads/2020/03/empathyintheworkplace.pdf.

24) Brenner, M. (2020, February 3). "The surprising link between empathy and innovation." Thrive Global. https://community.thriveglobal.com/the-surprising-link-between-empathy-and-innovation/.

25) Lesley University. "The psychology of emotional and cognitive empathy." https://lesley.edu/article/the-psychology-of-emotional-and-cognitive-empathy.

26) Mazza, M., Pino, M.C., Mariano, M., et al. (2014). "Affective and cognitive empathy in adolescents with autism spectrum disorder. *Frontiers in Human Neuroscience* 8: 791. http://doi:10.3389/fnhum.2014.00791.

27) King, M. (2021). *Social Chemistry: Decoding the Patterns of Human Connection.* New York: E.P. Dutton.

28) https://www.usip.org/sites/default/files/2017-01/Core%20Principles%20of%20Active%20Listening%20Handout.pdf.

29) Greenberg, D. M., Warrier, V., Abu-Akel, A., et al. (2023). "Sex and age differences in 'theory of mind' across 57 countries using the English version of the 'Reading the Mind in the Eyes' test." *Proceedings of the National Academy of Sciences.* https://doi.org/10.1073/pnas.2022385119.

30) Ford, A. (2016). Gender stereotyping may start as young as three months, study of babies' cries shows. University of Sussex. https://www.sussex.ac.uk/broadcast/read/35272.

31) Riess, H. (2017). "The science of empathy." *Journal of Patient Experience* 4(2):74–77.http://doi:10.1177/2374373517699267.

32) Brown, B. (2018, October 9). *Dare to Lead.* Random House.

33) Jampol, L., Rattan, A., and Wolf, E.B. (2023). "Women get 'nicer' feedback—and it holds them back." *Harvard Business Review* (25 January). https://hbr.org/2023/01/women-get-nicer-feedback-and-it-holds-them-back.

34) www.powherredefined.com.

35) White, J.D. (2022). "Former Jamba Juice CEO James D. White: Empathy Is a Skill That Can Be Taught." *Harvard Business Review* (1 December). https://hbr.org/2022/12/former-jamba-juice-ceo-james-d-white-empathy-is-a-skill-that-can-be-taught.

36) Kelley, T., and Kelley, D. (2013, October 15). *Creative Confidence.* Currency.

37) Ashkanasy, N.M., and Humphrey, R.H. (2011). "Current emotion research in organizational behavior." *Emotion Review* 3 (2): 214–224. https://doi.org/10.1177/17540739 10391684.

38) Branson, R. (2011). *Stripped Bare: Adventures of a Global Entrepreneur.* Penguin.

39) Google, re:Work, "Guide: Understanding Team Effectiveness" (accessed on May 10, 2023). https://rework.with google.com/print/guides/5721312655835136/.

40) Chiaet, J. (2013). "Novel finding: Reading literary fiction improves empathy." *Scientific American* (4 October). https://www.scientificamerican.com/article/novel-finding-reading-literary-fiction-improves-empathy/.

Chapter 5

1) Edelman. (2002). "2021 Edelman Trust Barometer." https://www.edelman.com/trust/2021-trust-barometer.

2) Glassdoor Team. (2021). "What job seekers really think about your diversity and inclusion stats." Glassdoor for Employers Blog (12 July). https://www.glassdoor.com/employers/blog/diversity/#:~:text=Job%20seekers%20look%20for%20an,evaluating%20companies%20and%20job%20offers.

3) Amazon Ads. (2022). "The power of purpose-driven brands." https://advertising.amazon.com/higher-impact.

4) Buonfantino, G. (2022). "New research shows consumers more interested in brands' values than ever." Google Cloud. https://cloud.google.com/blog/topics/consumer-packaged-goods/data-shows-shoppers-prioritizing-sustainability-and-values.

5) Bloom, J., Munson, R., Jaros, N.D., and Li, J. (2021). "Can the difference of one year move you years ahead?" EY (22 November). https://www.ey.com/en_us/wealth-asset-management/can-the-difference-of-one-year-move-you-years-ahead?WT.mc_id=10818147&AA.tsrc=paidsearch&gclid=CjwKCAiAk--dBhABEiwAchIwkZ4lxxtia6N6399W3I4CHxEbt-YWlPDHQ7IvWtO-CAlMNdGfpnfgUhoC3QkQAvD_BwE.

6) Deloitte Insights. (2020). "The social enterprise at work: Paradox as a path forward." https://www2.deloitte.com/content/dam/Deloitte/cn/Documents/human-capital/deloitte-cn-hc-trend-2020-en-200519.pdf.

7) Statistica. (2023). "Distribution of Google employees in the United States from 2014 to 2021, by ethnicity." https://www.statista.com/statistics/311810/google-employee-ethnicity-us/.

8) Google Diversity Annual Report. (2023). "Workforce Representation by Race / Ethnicity." https://about.google/belonging/diversity-annual-report/2023/static/pdfs/

google_2023_diversity_annual_report.pdf?cachebust= 2943cac. p.13.

9) Williams, J. (2021). "Target's black history month merchandise faces backlash: 'Pain, suffering and stereotypes.'" *Newsweek* (5 February). https://www.news week.com/targets-black-history-month-merchandise-faces-backlash-pain-suffering-stereotypes-1567183.

10) Duke Energy. (2021). "Company launches Duke Energy Sustainable Solutions—offering renewable energy, resiliency solutions for commercial customers nationwide." Press release (27 April). https://news.duke-energy.com/ releases/company-launches-duke-energy-sustainable-solutions-offering-renewable-energy-resiliency-solutions-for-commercial-customers-nationwide.

11) Macrotrends. (2023). "Duke Energy gross profits 2010–2022." https://www.macrotrends.net/stocks/charts/DUK/duke-energy/gross-profit.

12) Newland, S. (2018). "The power of accountability." AFCPE (3rd quarter). https://www.afcpe.org/news-and-publica tions/the-standard/2018-3/the-power-of-accountability/.

13) Ibid.

14) Laatikainen, T.E., Haybatollahi, M., and Kyttä, M. (2018). "Environmental, individual and personal goal influences on older adults' walking in the Helsinki metropolitan area." *International Journal of Environmental Research and Public Health* 16 (1): 58. http://doi:10.3390/ijerph16010058.

15) Marks, J. (2020). LinkedIn post. https://www.linkedin.com/ posts/judy-marks-otis_black-executives-are-sharing-their-experiences-activity-6682349165915193346-bSGz/.

16) Prince, C.J. "Judy Marks on why she elevated D&I to top priority at Otis Worldwide." https://chiefexecutive.net/ judy-marks-elevates-di-to-top-priority-at-otis-worldwide/.

17) Porath, Christine and Pearson, Christine. (2013, January-February). *The Price of Incivility*. Harvard Business Review. https://hbr.org/2013/01/the-price-of-incivility.

18) Lean In and McKinsey & Company. (2016). "Women in the workplace: 2016." https://wiw-report.s3.amazonaws.com/ Women_in_the_Workplace_2016.pdf.

19) Makoni, A. (2022). "Black and Latinx employees face bias in job performance feedback, study finds." People of Color in Tech (20 July). https://peopleofcolorintech.com/front/ black-and-latinx-employees-face-bias-in-job-performance- feedback-study-finds/.

20) Thomas, D.A. (2001). "Race matters." *Harvard Business Review* (April). https://hbr.org/2001/04/race-matters.

21) Brown, B. (2018). "Clear is kind. Unclear is unkind." Brené Brown (15 October). https://brenebrown.com/articles/ 2018/10/15/clear-is-kind-unclear-is-unkind/.

22) Edelman, R. (2022). "The gravitational force of Gen Z." Edelman. https://www.edelman.com/trust/2022-trust-baro meter/special-report-new-cascade-of-influence# :~:text=Edelman%20has%20been%20following%20 brand,brands%20based%20on%20their%20values.

23) Edelman. (2021). "Edelman Trust Barometer 2021." https:// www.edelman.com/sites/g/files/aatuss191/files/ 2021-03/2021%20Edelman%20Trust%20Barometer.pdf.

24) Salesforce. (2023). "Let's build a more inclusive workplace and world." https://www.salesforce.com/company/equality/.

25) Salesforce. (2022). "Business travel." https://stakeholder impactreport.salesforce.com/environment/emissions- reductions#business-travel.

26) Benioff, M. and Langley, M. (2019). *Trailblazer: The Power of Business as the Greatest Platform for Change.* New York: Simon & Schuster, p. 102.

27) Hyder, B. (2022). "2022 equal pay update: The Salesforce approach to fairness." Salesforce (30 March). https://www .salesforce.com/news/stories/2022-equal-pay-update-the- salesforce-approach-to-pay-fairness/.

28) Salesforce. (2022). "Salesforce announces record fourth quarter and full year fiscal 2022 results." Press release

(1 March). https://investor.salesforce.com/press-releases/press-release-details/2022/Salesforce-Announces-Record-Fourth-Quarter-and-Full-Year-Fiscal-2022-Results/default.aspx.

Chapter 6

1) Murthy, V. (2023). "Surgeon General: We Have Become a Lonely Nation. It's Time to Fix That." *The New York Times* (30 April). https://www.nytimes.com/2023/04/30/opinion/loneliness-epidemic-america.html.
2) Malesic, J. (2022). *The End of Burnout: Why Work Drains Us and How to Build Better Lives*. Oakland, CA: University of California Press.
3) Malesic, J. (2022). "Your work is not your god: welcome to the age of the burnout epidemic." *The Guardian* (6 January). https://www.theguardian.com/lifeandstyle/2022/jan/06/burnout-epidemic-work-lives-meaning.
4) Williams, J.C. (2020). "The pandemic has exposed the fallacy of the 'ideal worker.'" *Harvard Business Review* (11 May). https://hbr.org/2020/05/the-pandemic-has-exposed-the-fallacy-of-the-ideal-worker.
5) Reid, E., and Ramarajan, L. (2016). "Managing the high-intensity workplace." *Harvard Business Review* (June). https://hbr.org/2016/06/managing-the-high-intensity-workplace.
6) Duckworth, A.L. (2013). "Grit: The power of passion and perseverance." TED. https://www.ted.com/talks/angela_lee_duckworth_grit_the_power_of_passion_and_perseverance?utm_campaign=tedspread&utm_medium=referral&utm_source=tedcomshare.
7) Brant, J. (2020). "Entrepreneur of the year: Ping Fu." *Inc.* (6 February). https://www.inc.com/magazine/20051201/ping-fu.html.

8) Long Now. (n.d.). "People of Long Now: Ping Fu." https://longnow.org/people/ping-fu/#:~:text=Honored%20as%20Inc.,3D%20Systems%20in%20February%202013.

9) O'Brien, J. (2013). "Bend, not break: Leadership lessons for resilience amid struggle." *Fast Company* (3 January). https://www.fastcompany.com/3004166/bend-not-break-leadership-lessons-resilience-amid-struggle.

10) McClure, T. (2023). "Jacinda Ardern resigns as prime minister of New Zealand." *The Guardian* (18 January). https://www.theguardian.com/world/2023/jan/19/jacinda-ardern-resigns-as-prime-minister-of-new-zealand.

11) McGee, L., and Guy, J. (2023). "Nicola Sturgeon unexpectedly quits as first minister of Scotland amid swirl of political setbacks, citing 'brutality' of public life." CNN.com (15 February). https://www.cnn.com/2023/02/15/uk/nicola-sturgeon-resigns-scotland-intl/index.html.

12) Grant, N. (2023). "Susan Wojcicki, YouTube's longtime C.E.O., says she will step down." *The New York Times* (16 February). https://www.nytimes.com/2023/02/16/technology/susan-wojcicki-youtube-ceo-step-down.html.

13) Zimmerman, E. (2020). "What makes some people more resilient than others." *The New York Times* (21 June). https://www.nytimes.com/2020/06/18/health/resilience-relationships-trauma.html.

14) Sims-Schouten, W., and Gilbert, P. (2022). "Revisiting 'resilience' in light of racism, 'othering' and resistance." *Race&Class* 64(1):84–94. https://doi.org/10.1177/03063968221093882.

15) Hogg Staff. (2020). "Racial trauma and resilience in African American adults." Hogg Foundation for Mental Health (17 November). https://hogg.utexas.edu/racial-trauma-and-resilience-in-african-american-adults.

16) Lüdert, J. (2017). "Resilient leadership: A matter of authenticity." City University of Seattle (1 March). https://www.cityu.edu/resilient-leadership-a-matter-of-authenticity/.

17) Goleman, D., Sonnenfeld, J.A., and Achor, S. (2017). *Resilience*. Cambridge, MA: Harvard Business Review Press.

18) Coutu, Diane. (2020, May). *How Resilience Works*. Harvard Business Review. https://hbr.org/2002/05/how-resilience works.

19) Southwick, S.M., and Charney, D.S. (2018). *Resilience: The Science of Mastering Life's Greatest Challenges* (Chapter 4). New York: Cambridge University Press.

20) Yi, F., Li, X., Song, X., and Zhu, L. (2020). "The underlying mechanisms of psychological resilience on emotional experience: Attention-bias or emotion disengage ment." *Frontiers in Psychology* 11: 1993. http://doi:10.3389/fpsyg.2020.01993.

21) Zimmerman, E. (2020, June 21). "What makes some people more resilient than others." *The New York Times*.

22) Maul, S., Giegling, I., Fabbri, C., et al. (2020). "Genetics of resilience: Implications from genome-wide association studies and candidate genes of the stress response system in posttraumatic stress disorder and depression." *American Journal of Medical Genetics. Part B Neuropsychiatric Genetics* 183 (2): 77-94. http://doi:10.1002/ajmg.b.32763.

23) Rose, R. (2019). "How failure cultivates resilience." TEDx Manhattan Beach. https://www.ted.com/talks/raphael_rose_how_failure_cultivates_resilience.

24) Moore, C. (2023). "Resilience theory: A summary of the research" (+PDF). PositivePsychology.com (6 April). https://positivepsychology.com/resilience-theory/.

25) Levitan, D. (2015). "How to stay calm when you know you'll be stressed." TED. https://www.ted.com/talks/daniel_levitin_how_to_stay_calm_when_you_know_you_ll_be_stressed?language=en.

26) Zimmerman, E. (2020). "What makes some people more resilient than others." *The New York Times* (21 June).

27) Minter, H. (2014). "Six things I know: tech entrepreneur Ping Fu on why life is a mountain range." *The Guardian* (17 March). https://www.theguardian.com/women-in-leadership/2014/feb/17/ping-fu-tech-entrepreneur.

28) How I Built This. (2020). "How I built resilience: Morra Aarons-Mele." NPR (17 December). https://www.facebook.com/watch/live/?ref=watch_permalink&v=744321536201045.

29) Chowdhury, M.R. (2023). "The neuroscience of gratitude and effects on the brain." PositivePsychology.com (16 March). https://positivepsychology.com/neuroscience-of-gratitude/#:~:text=look%20beyond%20it.-,The%20Relationship%20Between%20Resilience%20And%20Gratitude, Gloria%20%26%20Steinhardt%2C%202016).

30) Rose, R. (2019). "How failure cultivates resilience." TEDx Manhattan Beach.

Chapter 7

1) Edelman. (2022). "Edelman Trust Barometer 2022." https://www.edelman.com/sites/g/files/aatuss191/files/2022-08/2022%20Edelman%20Trust%20Barometer%20Special%20Report%20Trust%20in%20the%20Workplace%20FINAL.pdf.

2) Maloney, D. (2019). "Transparency in business: the next wave in company evolution." Slack (30 November). https://slack.com/blog/collaboration/transparency-in-business-company-evolution.

3) Dixit, J. (2018). "Why transparency is the secret to improving employee experience." NeuroLeadership Institute (26 October). https://neuroleadership.com/your-brain-at-work/transparency-secret-employee-experience/?utm_term=&utm_campaign=Education+-+NA&utm_source=adwords&utm_medium=ppc&hsa_acc=6445333425&hsa_cam=15028076065&hsa_grp=130380740592&hsa_

ad=562239771740&hsa_src=g&hsa_tgt=dsa-390170176059 &hsa_kw=&hsa_mt=&hsa_net=adwords&hsa_ver=3&gclid =CjwKCAiA9NGfBhBvEiwAq5vSy-UD9Uy_12n50m_ Y6QXS8WEtacZ6OA6Wc5-EmR3Cjd1rEtG4x6HPWhoC90U QAvD_BwE.

4) Jones, E.E., and Kelly, J.R. (2010). "'Why am I out of the loop?' Attributions influence responses to information exclusion." *Personality and Social Psychology Bulletin* 36 (9): 1186–1201. https://doi.org/10.1177/0146167210380406.

5) Spangler, S. (2022). "Collaboration challenge for 2022—be intentional, transparent, and creative." McKinsey & Company (16 February). https://www.mckinsey.com/ featured-insights/in-the-balance/collaboration-challenge-for-2022-be-intentional-transparent-and-creative.

6) Warwick. "New study shows we work harder when we are happy." Press release. https://warwick.ac.uk/newsand events/pressreleases/new_study_shows/#:~:text=Happi ness%20makes%20people%20more%20productive, people%20around%2012%25%20more%20productive.

7) Great Place to Work. (2016). "The business case for high-rust culture." https://s3.amazonaws.com/media.greatplace towork.com/pdfs/Business+Case+for+a+High-Trust+Culture_081816.pdf.

8) Wang, Q., and Guan, Z. (2022). "Can sunlight disperse mistrust? A meta-analysis of the effect of transparency on citizens' trust in government." *Journal of Public Administration Research and Theory* muac040. https://doi .org/10.1093/jopart/muac040.

9) Edelman. (2022). "Edelman Trust Barometer 2022."

10) Dalio, R. (2017). "How to build a company where the best ideas win." TED. https://www.ted.com/talks/ray_dalio_ how_to_build_a_company_where_the_best_ideas_ win?language=en.

11) Ibid.

12) Ziemba, A. (2020). "How radical transparency can improve your business?" Boldare (22 September). https://www.boldare.com/blog/how-radical-transparency-can-improve-business/.

13) Edelman. (2018). "Two-thirds of consumers worldwide now buy on beliefs." Edelman News & Awards (2 October). https://www.edelman.com/news-awards/two-thirds-consumers-worldwide-now-buy-beliefs.

14) Ibid.

15) Vereckey, B. (2021). "BlackRock's Larry Fink: Don't divest fossil fuels, stay in the game." MIT Sloan School of Management (2 November). https://mitsloan.mit.edu/ideas-made-to-matter/blackrocks-larry-fink-dont-divest-fossil-fuels-stay-game.

16) Intel Newsroom. (2021). "Earth Day at Intel: Repair, reuse, recycle." Press release (22 April). https://www.intel.com/content/www/us/en/newsroom/news/earth-day-repair-reuse-recycle.html#gs.unzgu3.

17) Rodgers, S. (2019). "Editorial." Intel Newsroom (21 November). https://download.intel.com/newsroom/2021/archive/2019-11-21-editorials-intel-rule-action-improve-diversity-legal-profession.pdf.

18) Qualtrics. (2022). "For employees, shared values matter more than policy positions." Press release (2 June). https://www.qualtrics.com/news/for-employees-shared-values-matter-more-than-policy-positions/.

19) Glassdoor Team. (2021). "What job seekers really think about your diversity and inclusion stats." Glassdoor for Employers (12 July). https://www.glassdoor.com/employers/blog/diversity/.

20) Payscale. (2022). "How fair pay perception and pay transparency combat turnover." https://www.payscale.com/content/whitepaper/Fair-pay-perception-and-pay-transparency-combat-turnover.pdf.

21) Sull, D. and Sull, C. (2020). "How companies are winning on culture during COVID-19." *MIT Sloan Management Review* (28 October). https://sloanreview.mit.edu/article/how-companies-are-winning-on-culture-during-covid-19/.

22) Ibid.

23) Swinand, A. "Why transparency is critical to creating trust in an organization." The Trust Project at Northwestern University. https://www.kellogg.northwestern.edu/trust-project/videos/swinand-why-transparency-is-critical-to-creating-trust-in-an-organization.aspx.

24) Frei, F.X., and Morriss, A. (2020). "Begin with trust." *Harvard Business Review* (May-June). https://hbr.org/2020/05/begin-with-trust.

25) Airbnb News. (2020). "A message from co-founder and CEO Brian Chesky." Airbnb (5 May). https://news.airbnb.com/a-message-from-co-founder-and-ceo-brian-chesky/.

26) Leonard, J.H. (2022). LinkedIn post. https://www.linkedin.com/feed/update/urn:li:activity:6871807617849786368/?src=aff-ref&trk=aff-ir_progid.8005_partid.10078_sid._adid.449670&clickid=2SwVjRyhRxyNUtbz4oWQCVcdUkAyAi0hRV9a3I0&mcid=6851962469594763264&irgwc=1.

27) Anderson, R. (2022). "Woman goes viral for showing off tattoos in company headshot." GMA (18 January). https://www.goodmorningamerica.com/living/story/woman-viral-showing-off-tattoos-company-headshot-82203262.

28) Leonard, J.H. (2022). LinkedIn post.

Chapter 8

1) Catalyst. (2004). "The bottom line: Connecting corporate performance and gender diversity." https://www.catalyst.org/wp-content/uploads/2019/01/The_Bottom_Line_Connecting_Corporate_Performance_and_Gender_Diversity.pdf.

2) Dixon-Fyle, S., Dolan, K., Hunt, D.V., and Prince, S. (2020). "Diversity wins: How inclusion matters." McKinsey & Company (19 May). https://www.mckinsey.com/featured-insights/diversity-and-inclusion/diversity-wins-how-inclusion-matters.

3) Credit Suisse. (2019). "Gender diversity is good for business." Credit Suisse (10 October). https://www.credit-suisse.com/about-us-news/en/articles/news-and-expertise/cs-gender-3000-report-2019-201910.html.

4) Levine, S.R. (2020). "Diversity confirmed to boost innovation and financial results." *Forbes* (16 January). https://www.forbes.com/sites/forbesinsights/2020/01/15/diversity-confirmed-to-boost-innovation-and-financial-results/?sh=1a8c9ea9c4a6.

5) Lorenzo, R., Voigt, N., Tsusaka, M., et al. (2018). "How diverse leadership teams boost innovation." BCG (23 January).https://www.bcg.com/publications/2018/how-diverse-leadership-teams-boost-innovation.

6) Abouzahr, K., Krentz, M., Harthorne, J., and Taplett, F.B. (2018). "Why women-owned startups are a better bet." BCG (6 June). https://www.bcg.com/publications/2018/why-women-owned-startups-are-better-bet.

7) Carr, E.W., Reece, A., Kellerman, G.R., and Robichaux, A. (2019). "The value of belonging at work." *Harvard Business Review* (16 December). https://hbr.org/2019/12/the-value-of-belonging-at-work.

8) Cho, J.H. (2016). "Diversity is being invited to the party; inclusion is being asked to dance," Verna Myers tells Cleveland bar. Cleveland.com (25 May). https://www.cleveland.com/business/2016/05/diversity_is_being_invited_to.html.

9) Deloitte. (2019). "Uncovering talent: A new model of inclusion." https://www2.deloitte.com/content/dam/Deloitte/us/Documents/about-deloitte/us-uncovering-talent-a-new-model-of-inclusion.pdf.

10) Coqual. (2020). "New study examines why belonging at work is crucial during crisis." Press release (22 June). https://coqual.org/wp-content/uploads/2021/04/Power-Of-Belonging-1-Press-Release-Updated.pdf.

11) Kellerman, G.R., and Reece, A. "The value of belonging at work: Investing in workplace inclusion." https://grow.betterup.com/resources/the-value-of-belonging-at-work-the-business-case-for-investing-in-workplace-inclusion-event.

12) Brown, J. (2019). *How to Be an Inclusive Leader: Your Role in Creating Cultures of Belonging Where Everyone Can Thrive.* Berrett-Koehler Publishers, Inc, p. 5.

13) Cox, Gena. (2022, October 11). *Leading Inclusion.* Page Two.

14) Prismwork, "Modern Leadership 4 Men," January 2023. www.modernleadership4men.com.

15) Canadian Council for Refugees. (2023). "Anti-oppression." https://ccrweb.ca/en/anti-oppression.

16) Auger-Dominguez, D. (2022). "When your efforts to be inclusive misfire." *Harvard Business Review* (3 May). https://hbr.org/2022/05/when-your-efforts-to-be-inclusive-misfire.

17) Auger-Dominguez, D. (2023). LinkedIn post. https://www.linkedin.com/posts/daisyaugerdominguez_when-your-efforts-to-be-inclusive-misfire-activity-7030552414059397120-LqNL/?utm_source=share&utm_medium=member_ios.

18) Ibid.

19) Reiss, R. (2022). "I asked the world's top CEOs if they're taking diversity seriously. Here's why their answers could change your life." *Fortune* (23 November). https://fortune.com/2022/11/23/world-top-ceos-diversity-seriously-careers-workplace-leadership-robert-reiss/.

20) Stovall, J.M. (2023). "Diversity training does work. But only when you take these steps." *Fast Company* (23 January). https://www.fastcompany.com/90837549/diversity-training-does-work-but-only-when-you-take-these-steps.

21) The New Quo. (2023). "Meet Christina." https://www .thenewquo.com/meet-christina.

Chapter 9

1) Dhingra, N., Samo, A., Schaniger, B., and Schrimper, M. (2021). "Help your employees find purpose—or watch them leave." McKinsey & Company (5 April). https://www .mckinsey.com/capabilities/people-and-organizational-performance/our-insights/help-your-employees-find-purpose-or-watch-them-leave.

2) Khullar, D. (2018). "Finding a purpose for a good life. But also a healthy one." *The New York Times* (1 January). https:// www.nytimes.com/2018/01/01/upshot/finding-purpose-for-a-good-life-but-also-a-healthy-one.html.

3) Hill, P.L., and Turiano, N.A. (2014). "Purpose in life as a predictor of mortality across adulthood." *Psychological Science* 25 (7): 1482–1486. https://doi.org/10.1177/095679 7614531799.

4) Craig, N., and Snook, S.A. (2014). "From purpose to impact." *Harvard Business Review* (May). https://hbr.org/2014/05/ from-purpose-to-impact.

5) Gallup. (2023). "What is employee engagement and how do you improve it? 04 What are the drivers of employee engagement?" https://www.gallup.com/workplace/285674/ improve-employee-engagement-workplace.aspx#ite-357 473.

6) Craig, N. (2018). *Leading from Purpose: Clarity and Confidence to Act When It Matters Most*. New York: Hachette Books, p. 27.

7) Boseman, C. (2018). "Howard University Commencement Speech." YouTube video 0:31:50. https://www.youtube. com/watch?v=RIHZypMyQ2s.

8) *Greater Good Magazine.* (2023). "Purpose in life quiz." https://greatergood.berkeley.edu/quizzes/take_quiz/ purpose_in_life.

9) Brown, B. (2022). "Living into our values." BrenéBrown.com. https://brenebrown.com/resources/living-into-our-values/.

10) Laughton, M.B. (2022). "Athleta CEO: Women are driving the economy. It's time for businesses to prioritize them." CNN.com (8 March). https://www.cnn.com/2022/03/08/ perspectives/athleta-ceo-women-economy/index.html.

11) Athleta. (2021). "Words into action: 2021 update on our commitments." https://athleta.gap.com/browse/info. do?cid=1160634#:~:text=We%20committed%20to%20 Increase%20Representation,and%20to%20Recommit%20 to%20Community.

12) Athleta. (2023). "The Power of She Fund." https://athleta .gap.com/browse/info.do?cid=1175290.

13) B Lab. (2023). "Measuring a company's entire social and environmental impact." https://www.bcorporation.net/en-us/certification.

About the Authors

Lisen Stromberg

Lisen Stromberg is CEO of PrismWork, a culture innovation and leadership transformation consultancy providing c-suite executives, start-up entrepreneurs, and leaders across the globe with the data-driven insights and tools they need to achieve breakthrough success and impact. Lisen is also a best-selling author, award-winning independent journalist, and in-demand speaker who has been on stage at numerous high-profile conferences around the globe including SXSW, Cannes Lions, and at companies including Microsoft, Twitter, and many others. Her latest book, *Intentional Power: The 6 Essential Leadership Skills for Triple Bottom Line Impact*, provides leaders at every level with the tools and insights they need to drive better business results for the benefit of all stakeholders. She earned her BA at Dartmouth

College, has an MBA from UC Berkeley's Haas School of Business, and an MFA from Mills College. You can learn more about her at www.lisenstromberg.com.

JeanAnn Nichols

JeanAnn Nichols is an experienced executive coach, in-demand keynote speaker, and leadership instructor who aims to spark visionary, inclusive discussions that inspire positive change. She is especially passionate about empowering senior women and underrepresented minorities in technology industries to advance their careers. JeanAnn Nichols has effectively led and coached change in complex, multicultural, global corporate environments. She began her career as a manufacturing supervisor and process engineer, rising to the position of vice president and general manager at Intel Corporation. JeanAnn earned a BSc in Electrical Engineering from the University of Illinois, Urbana-Champaign, and an MBA from Santa Clara University in Santa Clara, California. She maintains a credential from the International Coach Federation and is a Certified Hudson Institute Coach. Her top-selling online course, "Be a Great Mentor: A Practical Guide to Mentorship" at Udemy.com, has over 20,000 enrolled students. JeanAnn serves on the Silicon Valley Board of How Women Lead, a nonprofit organization.

Capitalizing on the flexibility of a portfolio career, JeanAnn recharges by running, gardening, and traveling. She and her husband share a passion for hiking and classic cars.

Corey Jones

Corey Jones is a cofounder of PrismWork, an award-winning consultancy focused on cultural transformation through leadership development in the workplace. He brings over 20 years of leadership in the creative and innovation space to this conversation. As a leader, he's built diverse teams that flourished by focusing on cultures of empowerment and belonging. Corey is committed to conscious capitalism and currently serves as the committee chair for B Local Texas, a nonprofit to promote certified benefit corporations in the state. His insights give leaders the tools to connect cultural relevance to their brands' daily decisions with a vision of impact on tomorrow.

As a husband and homeschooling father, Corey continues to enjoy the thrill of life with his wife and three daughters in Texas.

Index